AN EXCERPT FROM
THE GOSPEL ACCORDING TO

LUKE

(CHAPTERS 22:39–24:53)

THE
PREACHER'S
OUTLINE &
SERMON
BIBLE®

NEW TESTAMENT

KING JAMES VERSION

Leadership Ministries Worldwide
Chattanooga, TN

I0190612

THE PASSION OF JESUS BOOKLET
KING JAMES VERSION

Copyright © 2004 by ALPHA-OMEGA MINISTRIES, INC.

All Rights Reserved

All other Bible study aids, references, indexes, reference materials
Copyright © 1991 by Alpha-Omega Ministries, Inc.

**All rights reserved. No part of this publication may be reproduced, stored
in a retrieval system, or transmitted in any form or by any means—electronic,
mechanical, photo-copy, recording, or otherwise—without the prior
permission of the copyright owners.**

Previous Editions of **The Preacher's Outline & Sermon Bible**®,
New International Version NT   Copyright © 1998
King James Version NT   Copyright © 1991, 1996, 2000
by Alpha-Omega Ministries, Inc.

Please address all requests for information or permission to:
Leadership Ministries Worldwide
PO Box 21310
Chattanooga, TN 37424-0310
Ph.# (423) 855-2181   FAX (423) 855-8616   E-Mail info@lmw.org
http://www.lmw.org

Library of Congress Catalog Card Number: 96-75921
International Standard Book Number: 978-1-57407-291-4

LEADERSHIP MINISTRIES WORLDWIDE
CHATTANOOGA, TN

Printed in the United States of America

5   6   7   8   9   14   15   16   17   18

DEDICATED

To all the men and women of the world who
preach and teach the Gospel of
our Lord Jesus Christ and
to the Mercy and Grace of God

&

- Demonstrated to us in Christ Jesus our Lord.

  "In whom we have redemption through His blood, the forgiveness of sins, according to the riches of His grace." (Ep.1:7)

- Out of the mercy and grace of God, His Word has flowed. Let every person know that God will have mercy upon him, forgiving and using him to fulfill His glorious plan of salvation.

  "For God so loved the world, that he gave His only begotten Son, that whosoever believeth in Him should not perish, but have everlasting life. For God sent not his son into the world to condemn the world, but that the world through him might be saved." (Jn.3:16-17)

  "For this is good and acceptable in the sight of God our Saviour; who will have all men to be saved, and to come unto the knowledge of the truth." (1 Ti.2:3-4)

The Preacher's Outline & Sermon Bible®

is written for God's servants to use in their study, teaching, and preaching of God's Holy Word…

- to share the Word of God with the world.
- to help believers, both ministers and laypersons, in their understanding, preaching, and teaching of God's Word.
- to do everything we possibly can to lead men, women, boys, and girls to give their hearts and lives to Jesus Christ and to secure the eternal life that He offers.
- to do all we can to minister to the needy of the world.
- to give Jesus Christ His proper place, the place the Word gives Him. Therefore, no work of Leadership Ministries Worldwide—no Outline Bible Resources—will ever be personalized.

ACKNOWLEDGMENTS AND BIBLIOGRAPHY

Every child of God is precious to the Lord and deeply loved. And every child as a servant of the Lord touches the lives of those who come in contact with him or his ministry. The writing ministries of the following servants have touched this work, and we are grateful that God brought their writings our way. We hereby acknowledge their ministry to us, being fully aware that there are many others down through the years whose writings have touched our lives and who deserve mention, but whose names have faded from our memory. May our wonderful Lord continue to bless the ministries of these dear servants— and the ministries of us all—as we diligently labor to reach the world for Christ and to meet the desperate needs of those who suffer so much.

THE GREEK SOURCES

Expositor's Greek Testament, Edited by W. Robertson Nicoll. Grand Rapids, MI: Eerdmans Publishing Co., 1970.

Robertson, A.T. *Word Pictures in the New Testament*. Nashville, TN: Broadman Press, 1930.

Thayer, Joseph Henry. *Greek-English Lexicon of the New Testament*. New York: American Book Co., n.d.

Vincent, Marvin R. *Word Studies in the New Testament*. Grand Rapids, MI: Eerdmans Publishing Co., 1969.

Vine, W.E. *Expository Dictionary of New Testament Words*. Old Tappan, NJ: Fleming H. Revell Co., n.d.

Wuest, Kenneth S. *Word Studies in the Greek New Testament*. Grand Rapids, MI: Eerdmans Publishing Co., 1966.

THE REFERENCE WORKS

Cruden's Complete Concordance of the Old & New Testament. Philadelphia, PA: The John C. Winston Co., 1930.

Josephus, Flavius. *Complete Works*. Grand Rapids, MI: Kregel Publications, 1981.

Lockyer, Herbert. *All the Books and Chapters of the Bible*. Grand Rapids, MI: Zondervan Publishing House, 1966.

_____. *All the Kings and Queens of the Bible*. Grand Rapids, MI: Zondervan Publishing House, 1961.

_____. *All the Men of the Bible*. Grand Rapids, MI: Zondervan Publishing House, 1958.

_____. *All the Miracles of the Bible*. Grand Rapids, MI: Zondervan Publishing House, 1961.

_____. *All the Parables of the Bible*. Grand Rapids, MI: Zondervan Publishing House, 1963.

_____. *The Women of the Bible*. Grand Rapids, MI: Zondervan Publishing House, 1967.

Nave, Orville J. *Nave's Topical Bible*. Nashville, TN: The Southwestern Company. Copyright © by J.B. Henderson, 1921.

The Amplified Bible. Scripture taken from *THE AMPLIFIED BIBLE*, Old Testament copyright © 1965, 1987 by the Zondervan Publishing House. *The Amplified New Testament* copyright © 1958, 1987 by The Lockman Foundation. Used by permission.

The Four Translation New Testament (Including King James, New American Standard, Williams - New Testament in the Language of the People, Beck - New Testament in the Language of Today.) Minneapolis, MN: World Wide Publications.

The New Compact Bible Dictionary, Edited by T. Alton Bryant. Grand Rapids, MI: Zondervan Publishing House, 1967.

The New Thompson Chain Reference Bible. Indianapolis, IN: B.B. Kirkbride Bible Co., Inc., 1964.

THE COMMENTARIES

Barclay, William. *Daily Study Bible Series*. Philadelphia, PA: Westminster Press, Began in 1953.

Bruce, F.F. *The Epistle to the Ephesians*. Westwood, NJ: Fleming H. Revell Co., 1968.

_____. *Epistle to the Hebrews*. Grand Rapids, MI: Eerdmans Publishing Co., 1964.

_____. *The Epistles of John*. Old Tappan, NJ: Fleming H. Revell Co., 1970.

Criswell, W.A. *Expository Sermons on Revelation*. Grand Rapids, MI: Zondervan Publishing House, 1962-66.

Greene, Oliver. *The Epistles of John*. Greenville, SC: The Gospel Hour, Inc., 1966.

_____. *The Epistles of Paul the Apostle to the Hebrews*. Greenville, SC: The Gospel Hour, Inc., 1965.

_____. *The Epistles of Paul the Apostle to Timothy & Titus*. Greenville, SC: The Gospel Hour, Inc., 1964.

_____. *The Revelation Verse by Verse Study*. Greenville, SC: The Gospel Hour, Inc., 1963.

Henry, Matthew. *Commentary on the Whole Bible*. Old Tappan, NJ: Fleming H. Revell Co.

Hodge, Charles. *Exposition on Romans & on Corinthians*. Grand Rapids, MI: Eerdmans Publishing Co., 1972-1973.

Ladd, George Eldon. *A Commentary On the Revelation of John*. Grand Rapids, MI: Eerdmans Publishing Co., 1972-1973.

Leupold, H.C. *Exposition of Daniel*. Grand Rapids, MI: Baker Book House, 1969.

Morris, Leon. *The Gospel According to John*. Grand Rapids, MI: Eerdmans Publishing Co., 1971.

Newell, William R. *Hebrews, Verse by Verse*. Chicago, IL: Moody Press, 1947.

Strauss, Lehman. *Devotional Studies in Galatians & Ephesians*. Neptune, NJ: Loizeaux Brothers, 1957.

_____. *Devotional Studies in Philippians*. Neptune, NJ: Loizeaux Brothers, 1959.

_____. *James, Your Brother*. Neptune, NJ: Loizeaux Brothers, 1956.

_____. *The Book of the Revelation*. Neptune, NJ: Loizeaux Brothers, 1964.

The New Testament & Wycliffe Bible Commentary, Edited by Charles F. Pfeiffer & Everett F. Harrison. New York: The Iverson Associates, 1971. Produced for Moody Monthly. Chicago Moody Press, 1962.

The Pulpit Commentary, Edited by H.D.M. Spence & Joseph S. Exell. Grand Rapids, MI: Eerdmans Publishing Co., 1950.

Thomas, W.H. Griffith. *Hebrews, A Devotional Commentary*. Grand Rapids, MI: Eerdmans Publishing Co., 1970.

_____. *Outline Studies in the Acts of the Apostles*. Grand Rapids, MI: Eerdmans Publishing Co., 1956.

_____. *St. Paul's Epistle to the Romans*. Grand Rapids, MI: Eerdmans Publishing Co., 1946.

_____. *Studies in Colossians & Philemon*. Grand Rapids, MI: Baker Book House, 1973.

Tyndale New Testament Commentaries. Grand Rapids, MI: Eerdmans Publishing Co., Began in 1958.

Walker, Thomas. *Acts of the Apostles*. Chicago, IL: Moody Press, 1965.

Walvoord, John. *The Thessalonian Epistles*. Grand Rapids, MI: Zondervan Publishing House, 1973.

"Woe is unto me, if I preach not the gospel"
(1 Co.9:16)

Dear Reader,

It is our sincere hope that this excerpt from *The Preacher's Outline and Sermon Bible, Vol.4, Luke*, will stir you to study, preach, or teach the *passion* of Christ with new fervor. Luke's account of Christ's crucifixion is unique in that it is the Gospel of Christ's passion, the death of the Son of Man for the sins of humanity. Perhaps your goal is to personally learn more about Christ's sacrificial death. Or maybe you want to help others understand the cross more clearly. Or possibly you will use it as a witnessing tool. Regardless, it is our prayer that *The Passion of Jesus* will be a true blessing to your life and to all those it touches.

May our Lord bring this, the greatest sacrifice of all times, alive in your heart!

Your fellow servants at...
Leadership Ministries Worldwide

OUTLINE OF LUKE
(*CHAPTERS 22:39–24:53*)

THE PREACHER'S OUTLINE & SERMON BIBLE® is *unique*. It differs from all other Study Bibles & Sermon Resource Materials in that every Passage and Subject is outlined right beside the Scripture. When you choose any *Subject* below and turn to the reference, you have not only the Scripture, but you discover the Scripture and Subject *already outlined for you—verse by verse*.

XI. THE SON OF MAN'S SUFFERINGS: HIS AGONY, TRIALS, AND CRUCIFIXION, 22:39-23:56

    A. Jesus' Great Agony: Bearing Unbelievable Weight, 22:39-46
       (Matthew 26:36-46; Mark 14:32-42; John 18:1; see Hebrews 5:7-8; 12:3-4)
    B. Jesus' Arrest: Terrible Sins Against Jesus, 22:47-53
       (Matthew 26:47-56; Mark 14:43-52; John 18:3-11)
    C. Peter's Denial: The Great Tragedy of Denial, 22:54-62
       (Matthew 26:57, 69-75; Mark 14:53-54; 66-72; John 18:15-18, 25-27)
    D. Jesus Tried Before the Sanhedrin Court: The Phenomenal Claims of Jesus, 22:63-71
       (Matthew 26:57-68; 27:1; Mark 14:53-65; 15:1; John 18:12-14, 19-24)
    E. Jesus' First Trial Before Pilate and Herod: The Shirking of Duty and Personal Concern, 23:1-12
       (Matthew 27:11-14; Mark 15:1-5; John 18:28-38)
    F. Jesus' Second Trial Before Pilate: The Tragedy of a Compromising Man, 23:13-25
       (Matthew 27:15-25; Mark 15:6-15; John 18:39-19:16)
    G. Jesus' Crucifixion and Its Events, 23:26-49
       (Matthew 27:26-56; Mark 15:16-41; John 19:16-37)
    H. Jesus' Burial: A Secret Disciple Stirred to Step Forth, 23:50-56
       (Matthew 27:57-61; Mark 15:42-47; John 19:38-42)

XII. THE SON OF MAN'S GLORY: HIS RESURRECTION AND ASCENSION, 24:1-53

    A. Jesus' Empty Tomb: Its Discovery, 24:1-12
       (see Matthew 28:1-15; Mark 16:1-11; John 20:1-18)
    B. Jesus' Appearance to Two Believers on the Road to Emmaus: An Immortal Journey, 24:13-35
       (Mark 16:12-13)
    C. Jesus' Appearance to the Disciples: The Great Statements of the Christian Faith, 24:36-49
       (Mark 16:14; John 20:19-23; 20:26-21:25)
    D. Jesus' Last Appearance: The Ascension, 24:50-53
       (Mark 16:19-20; Acts 1:9-11)

	XI. THE SON OF MAN'S SUFFERINGS: HIS AGONY, TRIALS, & CRUCIFIXION, 22:39–23:56	cast, and kneeled down, and prayed, 42 Saying, Father, if thou be willing, remove this cup from me: nevertheless not my will, but thine be done.	
	A. Jesus' Great Agony: Bearing Unbelievable Weight, 22:39-46 (Mt. 26:36-46; Mk. 14:32-42; Jn. 18:1; He. 5:7-8; 12:3-4)	43 And there appeared an angel unto him from heaven, strengthening him. 44 And being in an agony he prayed more earnestly: and his sweat was as it were great drops of blood falling down to the ground.	4. The awful weight of Jesus' intense agony[DS2] a. Seen in the angel's visit b. Seen in His intense praying c. Seen in His sweat
1. The setting: Jesus on the Mount of Olives a. His custom to withdraw there for prayer b. His disciples followed 2. The heavy weight of the trial about to be faced by the disciples 3. The painful weight of Jesus' own cup of suffering[DS1]	39 And he came out, and went, as he was wont, to the mount of Olives and his disciples also followed him. 40 And when he was at the place, he said unto them, Pray that ye enter not into temptation. 41 And he was withdrawn from them about a stone's	45 And when he rose up from prayer, and was come to his disciples, he found them sleeping for sorrow, 46 And said unto them, Why sleep ye? rise and pray, lest ye enter into temptation.	5. The tragic weight of the disciples' continued weakness

DIVISION XI

THE SON OF MAN'S SUFFERINGS: HIS AGONY, TRIALS, AND CRUCIFIXION, 22:39–23:56

A. Jesus' Great Agony: Bearing Unbelievable Weight, 22:39-46

(22:39-46) **Introduction**: this passage shows the great weight of suffering Jesus underwent in facing the cross.
1. The setting: Jesus on the Mount of Olives (v.39).
2. The heavy weight of the trial about to be faced by the disciples (v.40).
3. The painful weight of Jesus' own cup of suffering (vv.41-42).
4. The awful weight of Jesus' intense agony (vv.43-44).
5. The tragic weight of the disciples' continued weakness (vv.45-46).

1 (22:39) **Prayer—Jesus Christ, Prayer Life of**: Jesus entered the Mount of Olives. His disciples were with Him. The significant thing to note is this: it was His custom to seek time alone with God on the mount when in Jerusalem. During the last week of His life, He was spending every night in prayer (see note 2).

2 (22:40) **Jesus Christ, Sufferings—Discipleship**: Jesus bore the heavy weight of His disciples' great trial. The greatest trial the disciples were ever to know was at hand, and they did not know it. In just a few hours they were going to fall away. They desperately needed to pray that they "enter not into temptation" (v.40), that they not be so gripped by temptation and sin that they would be too weak to repent when Jesus arose and confronted them. Jesus knew the enormous temptation that was coming upon these men, and He loved and cared for them, so He was bound to feel the pressure of their trial.

> "For we have not an high priest which cannot be touched with the feeling of our infirmities; but was in all points tempted like as we are, yet without sin. Let us therefore come boldly unto the throne of grace, that we may obtain mercy, and find grace to help in time of need" (He.4:15-16).
> "For we wrestle not against flesh and blood, but against principalities, against powers, against the rulers of the darkness of this world, against spiritual wickedness in high places. Wherefore take unto you the whole armour of God, that ye may be able to withstand in the evil day, and having done all, to stand" (Ep.6:12-13).
> "Ye therefore, beloved, seeing ye know these things before, beware lest ye also, being led away with the error of the wicked, fall from your own stedfastness" (2 Pe.3:17).

3 (22:41-42) **Jesus Christ, Sufferings**: Jesus bore the painful weight of His own cup of suffering. In confronting death Jesus turned to God, crying with *strong cries and tears* (see Heb.5:7). Four things are seen in this verse.
1. Jesus got all alone and prostrated Himself before God. Luke says He withdrew "about a stone's cast" from the three disciples. Note two significant points. (1) He needed to be alone with God—He was desperate. (b) He fell on His face—the pressure and weight were unbearable.
2. Jesus prayed, "Father (pater)." It is the address of a child's love and dependency and trust. The child knows that His father will hear and turn to him when he calls "Father." But note also the words, "*O my* Father." Jesus was broken and weighted down; He had fallen prostrate upon the ground with His face buried in His hands. In desperation He cried out

"*O my* Father" (see Mt.26:39). Just like a child, He cried out to His Father in brokenness and dependency, knowing that His Father would hear Him and turn to help Him.

3. Jesus asked God to remove the cup from Him. (See DEEPER STUDY # 4, *Cup*—Mt.26:39. Also see DEEPER STUDY # 1—Mt.27:26-44; see Mt.20:19.) The human nature and will of Jesus is clearly seen in this experience. He was as much flesh as any man is; therefore, He begged God to choose another way other than the cup, if possible. The experience of being *separated from God* upon the cross was too much to bear.

4. The divine nature and will of Jesus is also clearly seen in this experience. Note the Lord's words: "Let this cup pass from me: nevertheless...." The first act, the first impulse and struggle of His will, had come from His flesh: to escape the cup of separation from God. But immediately, the second act, the second impulse and struggle of His will, came from His Godly nature: not to do as He willed, but as God willed.

Jesus' surrender to do God's perfect will in the Garden of Gethsemane was critical.

⇒ It was in His surrender that He was made perfect and was able to stand before God as the Ideal, Perfect Man.
⇒ It was in His surrender to be the Ideal, Perfect Man that His righteousness was able to stand for every man.
⇒ It was in His surrender to be the Ideal, Perfect Man that He was able to bear the cup of God's wrath against sin *for every man*.
⇒ It was in His surrender to be the Ideal, Perfect Man that His sacrifice and sufferings were able to stand for every man.

> **"But we see Jesus, who was made a little lower than the angels for the suffering of death, crowned with glory and honor; that he by the grace of God should taste death for every man. For it became him, for whom are all things, and by whom are all things, in bringing many sons unto glory, to make the captain of their salvation perfect through sufferings" (He.2:9-10).**

> **"Though he were a Son, yet learned he obedience by the things which he suffered; and being made perfect, he became the author of eternal salvation unto all them that obey him" (He.5:8-9).**

> **"For he hath made him to be sin for us, who knew no sin; that we might be made the righteousness of God in him" (2 Co.5:21).**

DEEPER STUDY # 1

(22:42) **Cup**: Jesus Christ was not fearing nor shrinking from death itself. This is clearly seen in Jn.10:17-18. Death for a cause is not such a great price to pay. Many men have died for causes fearlessly and willingly, some perhaps even more cruelly than Jesus Himself. Shrinking from betrayal, beatings, humiliation, and death—increased by foreknowledge—is not what was happening to Jesus. As stated, some men have faced such trials courageously, even inviting martyrdom for a cause. The Lord knew He was to die from the very beginning, and He had been preparing His disciples for His death (see DEEPER STUDY # 1—Lu.9:22). It was not human and physical suffering from which Jesus was shrinking. Such an explanation is totally inadequate in explaining Gethsemane. The great cup or trial Jesus was facing was separation from God (see note, pt.1—Mt.26:37-38). He was to be the sacrificial *Lamb of God* who was to take away the sins of the world (Jn.1:29). He was to bear the judgment of God for the sins of the world (see note—Mt.27:46-49; see Is.53:10). Jesus Himself had already spoken of the "cup" when referring to His sacrificial death (see DEEPER STUDY # 2—Mt.20:22-23; note—Mk.14:41-42; DEEPER STUDY # 2—Jn.18:11).

Scripture speaks of the cup in several ways.

1. The cup is called "the cup of the Lord's fury" (Is.51:17).
2. The cup is associated with suffering and God's wrath (see Ps.11:6; Is.51:17; Lu.22:42).
3. The cup is also associated with salvation. Because Jesus drank the cup of suffering and wrath for us, we can "take the cup of salvation and call upon the name of the Lord" (Ps.116:13). He bears the judgment of God for the sins of the world (Is.53:10).

---

4 (22:43-44) **Jesus Christ, Suffering**: Jesus bore the awful weight of intense agony. This is seen in three facts.

1. God had to send an angel to strengthen Jesus. What did the angel do? We are not told, but certainly the angel would have shared how His death...

• was an act that glorified and honored God because it was doing exactly what His Father wanted. It was an act of obedience, of love and adoration for God. It was an offering, the perfect offering to God (see note—Ep.5:2).
• was to result in His own glory and honor and exaltation (He.12:2; Ph.2:6-11).
• was the only way man could be saved eternally.

Also, the angel probably did some very practical things. We can imagine the angel's embracing His Lord, just holding Him ever so tightly, perhaps infusing strength into His being. The scene of our Lord's being so weak that He had to be embraced and engulfed in the arms of an angel should break the believer's heart. Perhaps the angel wiped the perspiration and blood and tears off His brow. Whatever the scene, we need to see the awful weight and intensity of our Lord's agony.

2. He prayed "more earnestly," more intensely. The reason is seen in the Greek words for "being in an agony" (genomenos en agonia). The Greek (aorist participle) means Jesus experienced a growing agony. The weight upon Him was not only intense, it grew more and more intense. The pressure and sense of suffering became heavier and heavier. The picture is that of His becoming engrossed and embodied in agony. Thus, He prayed more and more earnestly. His prayer grew and increased in intensity even as His agony intensified.

3. He sweat great drops of blood. The words *great drops* (thromboi) mean thick clots of blood. Apparently Jesus was under so much pressure the capillary veins right under the skin burst and the blood mingled with sweat and poured through the enlarged pores. What Jesus was experiencing can never be known (see DEEPER STUDY # 3, *Jesus Christ, Suffering*—Lu.22:43-44).

DEEPER STUDY # 2

(22:43-44) **Jesus Christ, Suffering**: words could never express what Jesus experienced. Words to describe the suffering of Jesus are totally inadequate. Using all the descriptive words in the world would be as inadequate as using a syringe to drain an ocean.

1. There was the *mental and emotional agony*: the weight, pressure, anguish, sorrow, and excessive strain such as no man has ever experienced. He was the Son of God, the Maker of heaven and earth; but *now* pressing in ever so heavily upon His mind and spirit were the images, the thoughts of...

- the *hardness and unbelief* of all men everywhere
- the *rejection* of His own people, the Jews
- the *malice* of the world's leaders, both Jew and Gentile, religious and civil
- the *betrayal* of one of His own, Judas
- the *desertion* of all His men
- the *denial* by the leader of His own men, Peter
- the *injustice and condemnation* of His trial
- the *ridicule and pain* of being scourged, spit upon, slugged, cursed, mocked, crowned with thorns, nailed to the cross and killed
- the *wrath of God* that was soon to be cast upon Him as the Sin-Bearer of the world
- the *departure of God's Spirit* from Him as He bore the sins of the world

2. There was the *physical experience of death while being the Son of God*. What was it like for the Son of God to die just as all men die? If just the physical aspect of Jesus' death is considered, His death was still different from all other men.

a. Jesus as the Son of God possessed the very seed of life within His being (see DEEPER STUDY # 1—Jn.17:2-3).

b. Jesus as the Son of God possessed no seed of death (Jn.14:6; 1 Ti.6:16; 1 Jn.1:1-2. See Jn.1:4.) But man does. Man possesses the seed of corruption and death; man's sinful nature knows nothing and expects nothing but death. However, the sinless nature of Jesus knew nothing of sin and death. Therefore, the agony and pain of death was bound to be as different from man's death as white is different from black.

There is another fact to note as well. Man suffers the depth of humiliation in death. No matter how much man struggles to live, he irrevocably wastes and wastes away until he is carried into the grave and dust of the ground. But not Jesus. Again He was sinless, perfect even in His human nature. Imagine the humiliation: the Son of God—Perfect Man, Perfect God—having to die upon this earth! No wonder He "began to be sorrowful and *very heavy*!" No wonder He could say, "My soul is exceeding sorrowful, *even unto death*." In some mysterious way, God made Jesus to become sin for us (2 Co.5:21).

3. There was *the spiritual experience of death* while being the Son of Man (see note—Mt.5:17-18; DEEPER STUDY # 3—8:20; DEEPER STUDY # 2—Ro.8:3). There is so much in this fact, yet so little can ever be known.

a. First, what is it like to be without sin? Although being fully man, Jesus was sinless. He lived as all men live facing all the trials and temptations that men face, yet He never sinned. He became the Perfect Man, the Ideal Man—all that God wants man to be. Therefore, He became the Pattern for all men.

> "For we have not an high priest which cannot be touched with the feeling of our infirmities; but was in all points tempted like as we are, yet without sin" (He.4:15; see 2 Co.5:21; 1 Pe.2:22; 1 Jn.3:5).
> "Though he were a Son, yet learned he obedience by the things which he suffered; and being made perfect, he became the author of eternal salvation unto all them that obey him" (He.5:8-9).

b. Second, what is it like to bear all the sins of the world? What is it like to be perfect and sinless, and then *all of a sudden* to have all the sins of the world laid upon Oneself? In some mysterious way, God took all the sins of the world and laid the whole *body of sin* upon Jesus. In some mysterious way, God made Jesus to become sin for us (2 Co.5:21). Jesus, as the Ideal Man, became the Ideal Sin-Bearer. He bore all the sins and all that sin causes, all the...

darkness	weight	worry	strife
pollution	pressure	guilt	warring
filth	anxiety	savagery	torture
dirt	turmoil	conflict	enmity
poison	corrosion	consumption	disturbance

> "All we like sheep have gone astray; we have turned every one to his own way; and the Lord hath laid on him the iniquity of us all" (Is.53:6).
> "In due time Christ died for the ungodly" (Ro.5:6).
> "For he hath made him to be sin for us, who knew no sin; that we might be made the righteousness of God in him" (2 Co.5:21).

3

> "So Christ was once offered to bear the sins of many; and unto them that look for him shall he appear the second time without sin unto salvation" (He.9:28).
> "Who his own self bare our sins in his own body on the tree, that we, being dead to sins, should live unto righteousness: by whose stripes ye were healed" (1 Pe.2:24).

c. Third, what is it like to bear all the judgment and condemnation of sin for all men? What is it like to be judged and condemned for *all the sins ever committed*? Jesus suffered for the sins of *the whole world*, suffered *separation* from God. The terrifying mystery of this hellish experience is seen in His cry upon the cross, "My God, My God, why hast thou forsaken me?" (See notes—Mt.27:26-44; 27:46-49; 1 Pe.2:21-25.)

> "But he was wounded for our transgressions, he was bruised for our iniquities: the chastisement of our peace was upon him; and with his stripes we are healed" (Is.53:5).
> "Christ hath redeemed us from the curse of the law, being made a curse for us: for it is written, Cursed is every one that hangeth on a tree" (Ga.3:13).
> "But we see Jesus, who was made a little lower than the angels for the suffering of death, crowned with glory and honor; that he by the grace of God should taste death for every man" (He.2:9).
> "For Christ also hath once suffered for sins, the just for the unjust, that he might bring us to God, being put to death in the flesh, but quickened by the Spirit" (1 Pe.3:18).

5 (22:45-46) **Jesus Christ, Suffering**: Jesus bore the tragic weight of the disciples' continued weakness. The disciples were weak, so weak in fact that they were of no help to Jesus as He faced the most severe crises of His life. Jesus had to face the cross knowing the terrible weakness of His own men. Note what happened.

1. Jesus arose from prayer and went to the three who were supposed to be praying with Him. They were asleep. The companionship and spirit of prayer and comfort He had sought were not there. All were asleep. He had been left alone to wrestle with God by Himself.

2. Jesus warned them of temptation. They had failed to pray for Him, but they must not fail to pray for themselves. Jesus said, "Watch and pray." Both were important. *Watchfulness* sees and *praying* prepares. They must watch in order to see temptation's coming, and they must pray in order to be prepared when temptation struck.

3. Jesus warned of the flesh and its weakness. They were sleeping because of the emotional strain and distress of the evening. As Luke says, they slept because of "sorrow," that is, sadness (Lu.22:45). The evening had been shocking and taxing. They were weary, fatigued, and preoccupied. Concentration in prayer was difficult. They probably fought to stay awake and to pray for their Lord, but the importance of prayer and of spiritual dependency upon God in facing trials had not yet been learned. They were making two mistakes common among believers.

   a. They were depending upon their own wisdom and strength instead of God's Spirit to fight whatever battles lay ahead.

   b. They were taking God's deliverance for granted instead of assuring themselves of His deliverance through the testimony of prayer. They believed Christ to be the Messiah; therefore, they believed that God was going to deliver them from the Romans no matter what. As carnal, fleshy men are apt to do, the disciples no doubt thought prayer mattered little. They were just presuming upon God, taking His deliverance for granted. What Jesus said was, "Watch and pray, for only as you watch and pray can you keep from falling when the trial comes."

A point needs to be noted here: watchfulness and prayer bear *testimony* to God. When men watch and pray, they demonstrate that dependency and trust in God are well founded. When God answers the prayers of men, He demonstrates that He loves and delivers those who truly look up to Him. Without watching and praying, God allows the disciples to fall in order to teach that dependency and trust in Him are absolutely essential.

4. They were failing to stay awake to pray, to watch and be watchful in prayer. Their spirits were not alive and alert enough to overcome the flesh. The drowsiness and slumber of the flesh were stronger than the spirit (see note, pt.2—Mt.26:42-44; see Ep.6:18).

> "Watch and pray, that ye enter not into temptation: the spirit indeed is willing, but the flesh is weak" (Mt.26:41).
> "Wherefore let him that thinketh he standeth take heed lest he fall" (1 Co.10:12).
> "Continue in prayer, and watch in the same with thanksgiving" (Col.4:2).
> "Be sober, be vigilant; because your adversary the devil, as a roaring lion, walketh about, seeking whom he may devour" (1 Pe.5:8).

	B. Jesus' Arrest: Terrible Sins Against Jesus, 22:47-53	sword?	
	(Mt. 26:47-56; Mk. 14:43-52; Jn. 18:3-11)	50 And one of them smote the servant of the high priest, and cut off his right ear.	a. They asked if they should take up the sword
		51 And Jesus answered and said, Suffer ye thus far. And he touched his ear, and healed him.	b. One disciple began fighting
1. Deserting Jesus: The betrayer's sin	47 And while he yet spake, behold a multitude, and he that was called Judas, one of the twelve, went before them, and drew near unto Jesus to kiss him.		c. Jesus rebuked the disciples
a. A professing disciple		52 Then Jesus said unto the chief priests, and captains of the temple, and the elders, which were come to him, Be ye come out, as against a thief, with swords and staves?	**3. Being blind to the Son of God: The religionists' sin**
b. A leader of sinners			
c. A deceptive follower	48 But Jesus said unto him, Judas, betrayest thou the Son of man with a kiss?		
2. Misunderstanding the Lord's will: The disciples' sin	49 When they which were about him saw what would follow, they said unto him, Lord, shall we smite with the	53 When I was daily with you in the temple, ye stretched forth no hands against me: but this is your hour, and the power of darkness.	**4. Joining forces with the power of darkness: The people's sin**

DIVISION XI

THE SON OF MAN'S SUFFERINGS: HIS AGONY, TRIALS, AND CRUCIFIXION, 22:39–23:56

B. Jesus' Arrest: Terrible Sins Against Jesus, 22:47-53

(22:47-53) **Introduction**: it took only a few minutes to arrest Jesus. However, in those few minutes was painted a dramatic picture of four terrible sins against the Lord, sins that are repeated by too many in every generation.
1. Deserting Jesus: the betrayer's sin (vv.47-48).
2. Misunderstanding the Lord's will: the disciples' sin (vv.49-51).
3. Being blind to the Son of God: the religionists' sin (v.52).
4. Joining forces with the power of darkness: the people's sin (v.53).

1 (22:47-48) **Unbelief—Desertion—Apostasy—Judas**: the sin committed by Judas was that of deserting the Lord and betraying Hum. Three things are seen in Judas' desertion.

1. He was a *professing* disciple, a man who claimed to be a follower of the Lord. In fact, he had actually been with the Lord and His followers for over two years. On this very evening, just a few hours before, he had been eating and fellowshipping with the Lord and the other disciples; but ever so quickly, he had turned away.

2. He was a *leader* of sinners, leading the world in its opposition to Jesus. Note the words "went before them." As pointed out earlier, he chose the world before Jesus—the world's money, position, and recognition (fame). (See note—Mk.14:10.)

The crowd which Judas led is identified by Matthew and Mark as being arresting officers or temple police from the Sanhedrin. John says they included Roman soldiers. Matthew and Mark say they were armed. The soldiers, of course, had their swords; the elders and other officials of the High Priest had armed themselves with boards and sticks (see Mt.26:47).

3. He had a *deceptive* commitment to the Lord. Note what happened. It was dark. How would the temple guards be able to recognize Jesus in the dark and keep Him from slipping away? Judas thought and came up with a plan. He would identify Jesus for them by walking up and greeting Jesus with a kiss. A kiss was a sign of friendship and commitment among people in the East, in particular among friends. Judas felt he could deceive the disciples; they would never suspect his sin.

What Judas planned, he did. The sin was bad, but the deception was worse. Jesus' question was searching: "Betrayest thou the Son of man with a kiss?" Note: the question was not a rebuke or reproach. Jesus was forcing Judas to think, to search his deceptive heart. He still wanted to reach Judas, if possible (see note—Mt.26:48-50).

Thought 1. How many profess Christ but do not really know Christ nor live for Christ? How many are deceivers just as Judas was: trying to make others think they are followers of Christ when they are really living *for themselves*? How many began to follow Christ but are now falling back into sin just as Judas did?

"**And they will deceive every one his neighbour, and will not speak the truth: they have taught their tongue to speak lies, and weary themselves to commit iniquity**" (Je.9:5).
"**The heart is deceitful above all things, and desperately wicked: who can know it?**" (Je.17:9).
"**That we henceforth be no more children, tossed to and fro, and carried about with every wind of doctrine, by the sleight of men, and cunning craftiness, whereby they lie in wait to deceive**" (Ep.4:14).
"**But evil men and seducers shall wax worse and worse, deceiving, and being deceived**" (2 Ti.3:13).
"**For there are many unruly and vain talkers and deceivers**" (Tit.1:10).
"**Take heed, brethren, lest there be in any of you an evil heart of unbelief, in departing from the living God**" (He.3:12).

"[These] shall receive the reward of unrighteousness, as they that count it pleasure to riot [party] in the day time. Spots they are and blemishes, sporting themselves with their own deceivings while they feast with you [the church]; having eyes full of adultery, and that cannot cease from sin; beguiling unstable souls: an heart they have exercised with covetous practices; cursed children" (2 Pe.2:13-14).

"For many deceivers are entered into the world, who confess not that Jesus Christ is come in the flesh. This is a deceiver and an antichrist" (2 Jn.7).

2 (22:49-51) **Flesh—Commitment—Carnal**: the sin committed by the disciples was that of misunderstanding the Lord's will. Note two things.

1. The disciples misunderstood the Lord's will and the spiritual nature of His kingdom. They were ready to *war in the flesh*. The disciple referred to in v.50 was Peter, and the servant whose ear was cut off was Malchus (Jn.18:10). Jesus restored the ear, miraculously healed it (Lu.22:51).

Peter thought the Messiah's hour had come, that Jesus was now ready to free Israel and establish the throne of David as the dominant nation in the world (see notes—Mt.1:1; DEEPER STUDY # 2—1:18; DEEPER STUDY # 3—3:11; notes—11:1-6; 11:2-3; DEEPER STUDY # 1—11:5; DEEPER STUDY # 2—11:6; DEEPER STUDY # 1—12:16; notes—22:42; Lu.7:21-23). Peter drew his sword (note he had one) and struck, slashing off the ear of Malchus.

2. Jesus rebuked the disciples: their carnal commitment, their warring in the flesh.
⇒ He told Peter to put his sword back into its sheath where it belonged (Mt.26:52).
⇒ He healed Malchus' ear (Lu.22:51).

The picture painted by the disciples' behavior is carnal commitment, that is, acting and struggling in the flesh. The disciples took their stand for Jesus *in the flesh*. Therefore they failed, and eventually they deserted Jesus. Acting in the flesh will always result in failing and deserting Christ. The disciples' carnal commitment is seen in four mistakes. Each mistake is too often seen in the life of believers.

1. The disciples misunderstood the Lord's Word. First, they thought Jesus was to establish an earthly kingdom. They thought in terms of the earthly, the physical, the material. Therefore, they *failed to grasp the spiritual and eternal kingdom* proclaimed by Jesus. Second, they never accepted the Lord's Word. Jesus had predicted His death and forewarned the disciples, giving them extensive training for months (see notes—Mt.16:13-20; 16:21-28; 17:1-13; 17:22; 17:24-27). Yet they refused to give up their preconceived ideas to accept what Jesus was saying. Therefore, they did not see the eternal world of the Spirit nor the eternal salvation which Jesus was securing.

2. The disciples did not wait for instructions from Jesus. They acted on their own, took matters into their own hands. The disciples had asked, "Lord, shall we smite with the sword?" But Jesus had not yet answered. However, this did not stop them; they went ahead and acted on their own.

Thought 1. How like so many of us! Too often, we act without waiting on the Lord.

3. The disciples did not ask Jesus what to do, not again and again. They did not *persist* until Jesus answered.

"Watch and pray, that ye enter not into temptation: the spirit indeed is willing, but the flesh is weak" (Mt.26:41).
"Watch ye therefore, and pray always, that ye may be accounted worthy to escape all these things that shall come to pass, and to stand before the Son of man" (Lu.21:36).
"Seek the LORD and his strength, seek his face continually" (1 Chr.16:11).

4. The disciples did not think clearly nor act wisely. Their actions could have led to the failure of God's will. It could have led to the death of many. That is what Jesus was saying: "Violence leads to violence. If you draw the sword, the soldiers will cut you down." Among God's people, the place of the sword is in the sheath, not drawn and slashing at people. God's people are to proclaim love and peace, not war and violence, not carnal and fleshly behavior.

"Not by might, nor by power, but by my spirit, saith the LORD of hosts" (Zec.4:6).
"As many as I love, I rebuke and chasten: be zealous therefore, and repent" (Re.3:19).
"But sanctify the Lord God in your hearts: and be ready always to give an answer to every man that asketh you a reason of the hope that is in you with meekness and fear" (1 Pe.3:15).

3 (22:52) **Sin—Unbelief—Blindness**: the sin committed by the religionists was that of being blind to the Son of God. The religionists refused to accept Jesus as the Messiah (see note and DEEPER STUDY # 1—Mk.14:1-2). The question of Jesus was piercing. Why did the world treat Him as a thief? They acted as though He stole from them. He did not preach a message that allowed them to live as they wished; it was as though He took the right to live as they wished away from them. He did not praise them, boost their egos, honor their service and gifts. Rather, He told them they were lacking in discernment and sinful, dying and doomed if they did not repent and begin to live as God said (see note—Mt.26:55-56).

Thought 1. Note a crucial point so often not seen. Jesus had to tell the truth in order for men to be saved. God is love, but His love is not like a grandfather's indulgence that accepts wrongdoing. His love is the father's ache and acceptance of repentance and obedience. *Only through repentance and obedience can a man ever know the love of God* (see Jn.14:21, 23-24; 15:10, 14). God does not accept a man who does wrong and lives unrighteously. Jesus had to tell men the truth, for He could not deceive men. If men wanted to be acceptable to God and live in His love, then they had to turn away from sin and come to God, believing that He exists and diligently seeking Him.

> **"But without faith it is impossible to please him: for he that cometh to God must believe that he is, and that he is a rewarder of them that diligently seek him" (He.11:6).**
> **"He that hath my commandments, and keepeth them, he it is that loveth me: and he that loveth me shall be loved of my Father, and I will love him, and will manifest myself to him" (Jn.14:21).**
> **"Jesus answered and said unto him, If a man love me, he will keep my words: and my Father will love him, and we will come unto him, and make our abode with him. He that loveth me not keepeth not my sayings: and the word which ye hear is not mine, but the Father's which sent me" (Jn.14:23-24).**
> **"If ye keep my commandments, ye shall abide in my love; even as I have kept my Father's commandments, and abide in his love....Henceforth I call you not servants; for the servant knoweth not what his lord doeth: but I have called you friends; for all things that I have heard of my Father I have made known unto you" (Jn.15:10, 14).**

4 (22:53) **Satan**: the people's sin was that of joining forces with the power of darkness. What Jesus said was alarming: "This is your hour, *and* the power of darkness." Those who opposed Jesus had joined forces with the power of darkness against Jesus. The power of darkness refers to the forces of evil, the evil one himself, Satan (Ep.6:12; Col.1:13). Note these points about the word "hour."

1. An hour is only a short time. It soon passes. Therefore, the power of darkness and those who oppose the Lord will last but a short time. Their hour will soon pass.

2. The power of darkness is always broken and conquered by light. When light appears, the presence and power of darkness are destroyed. So it is with God's Son, the Light of the world. The power of darkness and those who oppose Christ may have their hour now, but their hour is to end. He, the Light of the world, will arise and dispel the darkness and completely do away with it.

3. An hour soon passes, but then what is left? All the hours of life and of eternity. The power of darkness and those who oppose Christ may have an hour, but that will be all. However He, the Light of the world, will give Light to the world forever.

> **"For we wrestle not against flesh and blood, but against principalities, against powers, against the rulers of the darkness of this world, against spiritual wickedness in high places" (Ep.6:12).**
> **"Who hath delivered us from the power of darkness, and hath translated us into the kingdom of his dear Son: in whom we have redemption through his blood, even the forgiveness of sins" (Col.1:13-14).**

| 1. The cause of denial

  a. Following at a distance: Not staying close to Jesus
  b. Sitting in the midst of a crowd: Mingling with the world

2. The denial of pretension: Pretending not to know Jesus
  a. The charge: Had been seen with Jesus

  b. The denial: Pretended not to know Jesus | C. Peter's Denial: The Great Tragedy of Denial, 22:54-62
(Mt. 26:57, 69-75; Mk. 14:53-54, 66-72; Jn. 18:15-18, 25-27)

54 Then took they him, and led him, and brought him into the high priest's house. And Peter followed afar off.
55 And when they had kindled a fire in the midst of the hall, and were set down together, Peter sat down among them.
56 But a certain maid beheld him as he sat by the fire, and earnestly looked upon him, and said, This man was also with him.
57 And he denied him, saying, Woman, I know him | not.
58 And after a little while another saw him, and said, Thou art also of them. And Peter said, Man, I am not.
59 And about the space of one hour after another confidently affirmed, saying, Of a truth this fellow also was with him: for he is a Galilaean.
60 And Peter said, Man, I know not what thou sayest. And immediately, while he yet spake, the cock crew.
61 And the Lord turned, and looked upon Peter. And Peter remembered the word of the Lord, how he had said unto him, Before the cock crow, thou shalt deny me thrice.
62 And Peter went out, and wept bitterly. | 3. The denial of discipleship: Denying that one was a follower of Jesus

4. The denial of ignorance: Claiming to know nothing about what was being said
  a. The charge: Was a follower

  b. The emphatic denial: Knew nothing about Him

5. The answer to denial
  a. Remembering the Lord's word

  b. Getting alone
  c. Sensing godly sorrow*DS1* |

DIVISION XI

THE SON OF MAN'S SUFFERINGS: HIS AGONY, TRIALS, AND CRUCIFIXION, 22:39–23:56

C. Peter's Denial: The Great Tragedy of Denial, 22:54-62

(22:54-62) **Introduction**: denying Jesus is one of the greatest tragedies in all of life. Yet Jesus is denied often, not only by unbelievers but by believers as well. This passage is a study of denial, the awful tragedy of denying Jesus.

1. The cause of denial (vv.54-55).
2. The denial of pretension: pretending not to know Jesus (vv.56-57).
3. The denial of discipleship: denying that one was a follower of Jesus (v.58).
4. The denial of ignorance: claiming to know nothing about what was being said (vv.59-60).
5. The answer to denial (vv.61-62).

[1] (22:54-55) **Apostasy—Jesus Christ, Denied**: the cause of denial given in these verses is twofold. Peter failed Jesus and failed Him miserably.

1. "Peter followed afar off." *Following Jesus afar off* means not walking close to Him, not standing and being identified with Him. A man who follows *afar off* is not focusing on Christ. His mind and life are not fixed upon the Lord. His commitment is weak; therefore, he is easily…

- distracted by the world and drawn into its ways.
- stricken with fear—the fear of ridicule, embarrassment, abuse, persecution, being cut off, shunned, ignored, ostracized.

> **"For God hath not given us the spirit of fear; but of power, and of love, and of a sound mind. Be not thou therefore ashamed of the testimony of our Lord" (2 Ti.1:7-8).**

2. Peter "sat down among" the crowd, the crowd which represented the world of rejecters. Very frankly, Peter was failing Jesus miserably. Sitting down among the crowd was the last place he should have been. He, of course, should have never forsaken Jesus. But having fled, he should have been off alone with God in prayer, seeking answers and understanding from God (see notes—Mt.26:51-52; 26:55-56). Or he should have been with the other apostles, leading them to seek the face of God for understanding and direction.

> **"Wherefore come out from among them, and be ye separate, saith the Lord, and touch not the unclean thing; and I will receive you, and will be a Father unto you, and ye shall be my sons and daughters, saith the Lord Almighty" (2 Co.6:17-18).**

[2] (22:56-57) **Apostasy—Jesus Christ, Denied**: there was the denial of pretension—pretending not to know Jesus. When confronted, this denial says, "I have nothing to do with Christ."

Note what happened. A maid "earnestly looked" at Peter. She stared at him, observed him closely, thinking she had seen him with Jesus. She concluded that Peter was one of the Lord's followers: "This man was also with Him." There seems to be no threat or danger in this statement to Peter. At worst it seems that it would have led only to some bantering fsand ridicule. The rejecters standing around were naturally bantering back and forth about Jesus and His claims, considering Him to have been a fool. Peter had an opportunity, perhaps, to be a witness for Jesus, humbly sharing about the love and enormous care of Jesus for people. Perhaps he could have helped to turn some who were standing there to Jesus, or at least stopped some of the mob's ridiculing. We must always remember that John was somewhere in the palace as well, and as far as we know, he was maintaining his composure and testimony for Jesus.

Peter cracked under his fear. He denied Jesus, pretending he did not know Him or have anything to do with Him.

Thought 1. Weak believers fear the crowd. When in church they readily profess Christ, but out in the world, at work or at school, they fear being known as believers. They pretend not to know Christ.

"**But whosoever shall deny me before men, him will I also deny before my Father which is in heaven**" (Mt.10:33).
"**A false witness shall not be unpunished; and he that speaketh lies shall not escape**" (Pr.19:5).
"**But sanctify the Lord God in your hearts: and be ready always to give an answer to every man that asketh you a reason of the hope that is in you with meekness and fear**" (1 Pe.3:15).

3 (22:58) **Apostasy—Jesus Christ, Denied**: there was the denial of discipleship—denying that one was a follower of Jesus. When confronted, this denial is more emphatic and vocal, "I am not a disciple, not a follower of Christ."
Note the charge: "Thou art also *of them.*" The charge was true.
⇒ Peter had been with Jesus. He was an apostle; in fact, he was the leader of the apostles.
⇒ Peter was the disciple who had professed that Jesus was the Christ, the Son of God (Mt.16:16).
⇒ Peter was the disciple who had sworn loyalty to Jesus even if it meant death (Mt.26:33-35).

Peter emphatically denied that he was a disciple, a follower of Jesus: "I am not!" Peter was falling (progressing) more and more into sin. He was denying Jesus because he was not by His side, but *standing among* the Lord's rejecters.
⇒ He was standing among the Lord's rejecters because he had fled the Lord.
⇒ He had fled the Lord because he had acted in the flesh (see note—Lu.22:49-51).
⇒ He had acted in the flesh because he had not accepted the Lord's words for what they said.

"**Whosoever therefore shall be ashamed of me and of my words in this adulterous and sinful generation; of him also shall the Son of man be ashamed, when he cometh in the glory of his Father with the holy angels**" (Mk.8:38).
"**Be not thou therefore ashamed of the testimony of our Lord, nor of me his prisoner: but be thou partaker of the afflictions of the gospel according to the power of God**" (2 Ti.1:8).
"**Be strong and of a good courage, fear not, nor be afraid of them: for the LORD thy God, he it is that doth go with thee; he will not fail thee, nor forsake thee**" (De.31:6).

4 (22:59-60) **Apostasy—Jesus Christ, Denied**: there was denial of ignorance—claiming to know nothing about what was being said. This is the denial that claims ignorance, "I do not know what you are talking about; I know absolutely nothing about the matter." Matthew and Mark say Peter began to curse and swear, *denying any knowledge whatsoever about Jesus.*
Note: this accuser is sure Peter was a follower of Jesus. The man "confidently affirmed," insisted upon the fact. He even identified Peter's nationality, a Galilaean Jew. It was common knowledge that Jesus' disciples were Galilaeans.
Peter's chest was bound to be pounding with emotion and fear. His thoughts were flying, trying to figure how to escape. His emotions just burst forth in cursing and swearing, a forceful denial: "I know not what thou sayest." Note that this denial occurred about one hour after the last one. Peter's failure was a deteriorating failure.
⇒ At first, he pretended not to know Jesus.
⇒ Then he fell even farther. He emphatically denied being a disciple.
⇒ Now, he claimed total ignorance of all. He cursed and swore that he knew absolutely nothing about Jesus.

This is the point: Peter stayed in the crowd, still stood around the rejecters of Jesus—even after they had led him to deny Jesus twice. He was trying to be *of the world,* one of the crowd, when he should have been off praying and seeking to understand the ways of God.

"**Enter not into the path of the wicked, and go not in the way of evil men**" (Pr.4:14).
"**Ye therefore, beloved, seeing ye know these things before, beware lest ye also, being led away with the error of the wicked, fall from your own stedfastness**" (2 Pe.3:17).
"**They profess that they know God; but in works they deny him, being abominable, and disobedient, and unto every good work reprobate**" (Tit.1:16).
"**If we suffer, we shall also reign with him: if we deny him, he also will deny us**" (2 Ti.2:12).
"**And in nothing terrified by your adversaries: which is to them an evident token of perdition, but to you of salvation, and that of God**" (Ph.1:28).
"**And with many other words did he testify and exhort, saying, Save yourselves from this untoward generation**" (Ac.2:40).

5 (22:60-62) **Repentance—Confession**: there was three steps involved in Peter's repentance.

1. Remembering the Lord's words. Apparently while the rooster was crowing, the Lord, standing in the chamber of the palace, turned around and caught the eye of Peter (Lu.22:61). And Peter, eye to eye with the Lord, remembered the words the Lord had spoken to him:

> "And the Lord said, Simon, Simon, behold, Satan hath desired to have you, that he may sift you as wheat: but I have prayed for thee, that thy faith fail not: and when thou art converted, strengthen thy brethren" (Lu.22:31-32).

In the midst of all His own pain and suffering, the Lord's look told Peter that His Lord had not forgotten him. The Lord still loved and cared for Him and wanted his loyalty and service. Jesus had prayed for Peter, and the power of that prayer was now moving in Peter's heart and life. Peter now remembered His Lord's word and that word began to take effect.

2. Getting alone. Peter left as fast as he safely could from the porch or courtyard through the gate out into the night to get alone at last with God. He was broken, full of anguish and pain for having failed his Lord: he "wept bitterly."

3. Expressing godly sorrow: repentance (see DEEPER STUDY # 1—2 Co.7:10).

> "If we confess our sins, he is faithful and just to forgive us our sins, and to cleanse us from all unrighteousness" (1 Jn.1:9).
> "Repent therefore of this thy wickedness, and pray God, if perhaps the thought of thine heart may be forgiven thee" (Ac.8:22).
> "And said, O my God, I am ashamed and blush to lift up my face to thee, my God: for our iniquities are increased over our head, and our trespass is grown up unto the heavens" (Ezr.9:6).
> "Now therefore make confession unto the LORD God of your fathers, and do his pleasure: and separate yourselves from the people of the land" (Ezr.10:11).
> "For mine iniquities are gone over mine head: as an heavy burden they are too heavy for me" (Ps.38:4).
> "For I acknowledge my transgressions: and my sin is ever before me" (Ps.51:3).
> "Thus my heart was grieved, and I was pricked in my reins" (Ps.73:21; see Jn.16:8).
> "He that covereth his sins shall not prosper: but whoso confesseth and forsaketh them shall have mercy" (Pr.28:13).
> "Only acknowledge thine iniquity, that thou hast transgressed against the LORD thy God, and hast scattered thy ways to the strangers under every green tree, and ye have not obeyed my voice, saith the LORD" (Je.3:13).

DEEPER STUDY # 1
(22:62) **Repentance**: see note and DEEPER STUDY # 1—Ac.17:29-30.

1. The attitude of religion & the world toward the claims of Jesus	D. Jesus Tried Before the Sanhedrin Court: The Phenomenal Claims of Jesus, 22:63-71	and the chief priests and the scribes came together, and led him into their council, saying,	2. The first claim: He is the Messiah
	(Mt. 26:57-68; 27:1; Mk. 14:53-65; 15:1; Jn. 18:12-14, 19-24)	67 Art thou the Christ? tell us. And he said unto them, If I tell you, ye will not believe:	
a. There was physical & verbal abuse	63 And the men that held Jesus mocked him, and smote him,	68 And if I also ask you, ye will not answer me, nor let me go.	
	64 And when they had blindfolded him, they struck him on the face, and asked him, saying, Prophesy, who is it that smote thee?	69 Hereafter shall the Son of man sit on the right hand of the power of God.	3. The second claim: He is the Son of Man—who will be exalted to the right hand of God
	65 And many other things blasphemously spake they against him.	70 Then said they all, Art thou then the Son of God? And he said unto them, Ye say that I am.	4. The third claim: He is the Son of God
b. There was legal abuse—a formal trial[DS1]	66 And as soon as it was day, the elders of the people	71 And they said, What need we any further witness? for we ourselves have heard of his own mouth.	5. The conclusion: The claims were understood but rejected

DIVISION XI

THE SON OF MAN'S SUFFERINGS: HIS AGONY, TRIALS, AND CRUCIFIXION, 22:39–23:56

D. Jesus Tried Before the Sanhedrin Court: The Phenomenal Claims of Jesus, 22:63-71

(22:63-71) **Introduction**: this is the first trial of Jesus covered by Luke. The thrust of the trial was the phenomenal claims of Jesus, claims which demand a decision from every man.

1. The attitude of religion and the world toward claims of Jesus (vv.63-66).
2. The first claim: He is the Messiah (vv.67-68).
3. The second claim: He is the Son of Man—who will be exalted to the right hand of God (v.69).
4. The third claim: He is the Son of God (v.70).
5. The conclusion: the claims were understood but rejected (v.71).

1 (22:63-66) **World, Response to Jesus—Persecution, of Jesus Christ—Jesus Christ, Trials of**: the attitude of religion and the world to Jesus' claims was that of opposition. This is clearly seen in the treatment of Jesus during the night while He was being held for trial the next morning.

1. There was (and is today) physical and verbal abuse. They ridiculed and mocked and shamed and beat Him. Why? Because of His claims.

> **"Remember the word that I said unto you, The servant is not greater than his lord. If they have persecuted me, they will also persecute you; if they have kept my saying, they will keep yours also" (Jn.15:20. Also refer to Jn.15:20-25.)**

2. There was ridicule of His spiritual power. If He were the Son of God, He should know all things, so they mocked and challenged His power: "Prophesy, who is it that smote thee?" But God gives no signs, not to the mocking and obstinate and devilish unbeliever. (See note—Mk.8:12.)

3. There were all kinds of blasphemy and cursing spoken against Him. (How tragic! Yet, how much like men today!)

Note the setting for the formal trial of Jesus. This was a trial by the Sanhedrin, the ruling body of the Jews which included both religious and lay leaders (see DEEPER STUDY # 1, *Sanhedrin*—Mt.26:59). Jesus stood before them all on trial for His life. Note the words "came together": they gathered, resorted, *flocked together* just as a body of vultures over their prey. There is also the idea of accompanying. The picture is that of the Jewish leaders flocking or herding together around Jesus, of being called to accompany one another to their respective seats, ready to pounce on Jesus. There is no question about the evil of their hearts. They *were* ready to pounce on and eliminate Him.

The court was stacked against Jesus. The leaders, both lay and religious, had already *determined* to reject and oppose Him. He was a threat to both their nation and their personal security and position. They feared the loss of both, so they were set on killing Him. (For a discussion of the reasons for their opposition, see notes—Mt.12:1-8; note and DEEPER STUDY # 1—12:10; note—15:1-20; DEEPER STUDY # 2—15:6-9; DEEPER STUDY # 3—16:12.)

Thought 1. The religionists rejected and opposed Christ for two primary reasons, the same two reasons that men reject and oppose Him today.

1) Men are unwilling to deny self, to surrender all they are and have to Christ. They fear the loss of some-thing—some security, money, position, power, or pleasure. They love the world and self more than they are willing to love God.

2) Men are unwilling to deny their institutional religion: their religious practices that are *man-made*, *man-conceived*, *man-honoring*.

Thought 2. Men do *flock together* to oppose Christ. It is easier to oppose Him in the presence of others.

"Beloved, follow not that which is evil, but that which is good. He that doeth good is of God: but he that doeth evil hath not seen God" (3 Jn.11).
"Therefore to him that knoweth to do good, and doeth it not, to him it is sin" (Js.4:17).

DEEPER STUDY # 1

(22:66-71) **Jesus, Trials of**: there were at least six trials.
   1. An informal trial during the night before Annas (Jn.18:12-14, 19-23).
   2. An informal trial by night before Caiaphas and some Sanhedrin officials to find a charge against Jesus (Mt.26:57-68; Mk.14:53-65; Lu.22:54, 63-65).
   3. An early morning formal trial before a quickly assembled Sanhedrin to secure the verdict of the full Sanhedrin and to formulate the charge against Jesus (Mt.27:1; Mk.15:1; Lu.22:66-71).
   4. A preliminary questioning by Pilate (Mt.27:2, 11-14; Mk.15:1-5; Lu.23:1-5; Jn.18:28-38).
   5. A preliminary questioning by Herod (Lu.23:6-12).
   6. The formal Roman trial before Pilate (Mt.27:15-26; Mk.15:6-15; Lu.23:13-25; Jn.18:39-40).

The other events following Jesus' arrest seem to be:
   1. Peter's denial (Mt.26:58, 69-75; Mk.14:54, 66-72; Lu.22:54-62; Jn.18:15-18, 25-27).
   2. Judas' suicide (Mt.27:3-10; Ac.1:18-19). Both of these events took place between the first and second trial.
   3. Jesus crowned with thorns and severely beaten by the Roman soldiers (Mt.27:27-30; Mk.15:16-19; Jn.19:1-3).
   4. Simon's carrying Jesus' cross (Mt.27:31-32; Mk.15:20-21; Lu.23:26).
   5. Jesus' warning the women of the coming judgment upon Jerusalem (Lu.23:27-31). (See note—Mt.26:57; 26:59.)

---

2 (22:67-68) **Jesus Christ, Claims**: Jesus claimed to be the Messiah. The council did not come right out and accuse Jesus. They wanted Him to incriminate Himself; therefore, they questioned Him: "Art thou the Christ [Messiah]? Tell us." But Jesus could not answer, not directly. Note two facts.
   1. They did not understand the true Messiahship of God. God's Messiahship is spiritual and eternal, not physical and material (see note—Ep.1:3). Jesus had come to save men spiritually, not materially. Therefore if He told them, they would not believe; and if He asked them questions which would lead them to the truth, they would not answer. He had done this often (Lu.20:7, 26, 40).
   2. Jesus did not deny His Messiahship. The way He answered the council was an affirmation. Note His exact words, "If I *tell you*, ye will not believe." It was as though He said, "I am, but if I tell you, declare it vocally, you will not believe it." (See notes—Mt.1:1; DEEPER STUDY # 2—1:18; note—Lu.19:36-38 see Mk.11:1-11 for concepts of Messiah.)

"The woman saith unto him, I know that Messias cometh, which is called Christ: when he is come, he will tell us all things. Jesus saith unto her, I that speak unto thee am he" (Jn.4:25-26).
"Then said Jesus unto them, When ye have lifted up the Son of man, then shall ye know that I am he, and that I do nothing of myself; but as my Father hath taught me, I speak these things. And he that sent me is with me: the Father hath not left me alone; for I do always those things that please him" (Jn.8:28-29).

3 (22:69) **Jesus Christ, Claims**: Jesus claimed to be the Son of Man who will be exalted. Jesus was really making three claims.
   1. That He is the Son of Man (see notes—Lu.4:20-21; Jn.1:51; DEEPER STUDY # 3—Mt.8:20. See Da.7:13-14.)
   2. That He will not remain dead even if they kill Him. He will be raised into God's presence.
   3. That He will be exalted to sit on the right hand of the power of God.

"And declared to be the Son of God with power, according to the spirit of holiness, by the resurrection from the dead" (Ro.1:4).
"This Jesus hath God raised up, whereof we all are witnesses. Therefore being by the right hand of God exalted, and having received of the Father the promise of the Holy Ghost, he hath shed forth this, which ye now see and hear. For David is not ascended into the heavens: but he saith himself, The LORD said unto my Lord, Sit thou on my right hand, until I make thy foes thy footstool. Therefore let all the house of Israel know assuredly, that God hath made that same Jesus, whom ye have crucified, both Lord and Christ (Ac.2:32-36).
"And what is the exceeding greatness of his power to usward who believe, according to the working of his mighty power, which he wrought in Christ, when he raised him from the dead, and set him at his own right hand in the heavenly places, far above all principality, and power, and might, and dominion, and every name that is named, not only in this world, but also in that which is to come" (Ep.1:19-21).
"Wherefore God also hath highly exalted him, and given him a name which is above every name: that at the name of Jesus every knee should bow, of things in heaven, and things in earth, and things under the earth; and that every tongue should confess that Jesus Christ is Lord, to the glory of God the Father" (Ph.2:9-11).

4 (22:70) **Jesus Christ, Claims**: Jesus claimed to be the Son of God. Note several facts.

1. "They all" now questioned Jesus. The picture is that of an outroar, voices reacting to His claim to be the Son of Man, voices bursting forth together shouting: "Art thou then the Son of God?"

2. The definite article "*the*" is important. They were not asking if He were *a* son of God like many men claim. They asked if He were "*the* Son of God."

3. Jesus unquestionably claimed to be "*the* Son of God." (See note—Mk.14:62 for more discussion.)

> "Then they that were in the ship came and worshipped him, saying, Of a truth thou art the Son of God" (Mt.14:33).
>
> "The beginning of the gospel of Jesus Christ, the Son of God" (Mk.1:1).
>
> "And I [John the Baptist] saw, and bare record that this is the Son of God" (Jn.1:34).
>
> "For God so loved the world, that he gave his only begotten Son, that whosoever believeth in him should not perish, but have everlasting life. For God sent not his Son into the world to condemn the world; but that the world through him might be saved. He that believeth on him is not condemned: but he that believeth not is condemned already, because he hath not believed in the name of the only begotten Son of God" (Jn.3:16-18).
>
> "Jesus heard that they had cast him out; and when he had found him, he said unto him, Dost thou believe on the Son of God? He answered and said, Who is he, Lord, that I might believe on him? And Jesus said unto him, Thou hast both seen him, and it is he that talketh with thee" (Jn.9:35-37).
>
> "Say ye of him, whom the Father hath sanctified, and sent into the world, Thou blasphemest; because I said, I am the Son of God?" (Jn.10:36).
>
> "Jesus said unto her, I am the resurrection, and the life: he that believeth in me, though he were dead, yet shall he live: and whosoever liveth and believeth in me shall never die. Believest thou this? She saith unto him, Yea, Lord: I believe that thou art the Christ, the Son of God, which should come into the world" (Jn.11:25-27).
>
> "Of how much sorer punishment, suppose ye, shall he be thought worthy, who hath trodden under foot the Son of God, and hath counted the blood of the covenant, wherewith he was sanctified, an unholy thing, and hath done despite unto the Spirit of grace?" (He.10:29).
>
> "Whosoever shall confess that Jesus is the Son of God, God dwelleth in him, and he in God" (1 Jn.4:15).

5 (22:71) **Jesus Christ, Claims**: the claim of Jesus was understood, but the leaders rejected His claim. Jesus had both accepted and claimed the charge being made against Him. He was...

* The Messiah
* The Son of God
* The Son of Man

They had heard enough. In their obstinate unbelief, they condemned Him to death—condemned the Man who had come to save the world from its terrible plight of sin and death, from its desperate need for health and love and for salvation and life.

> "Even as the Son of man came not to be ministered unto, but to minister, and to give his life a ransom for many" (Mt.20:28).
>
> "For the Son of man is come to seek and to save that which was lost" (Lu.19:10).

	CHAPTER 23 **E. Jesus' First Trial Before Pilate & Herod: The Shirking of Duty & of Personal Concern, 23:1-12** *(Mt. 27:11-14; Mk. 15:1-5; Jn. 18:28-38)*	6 When Pilate heard of Galilee, he asked whether the man were a Galilaean. 7 And as soon as he knew that he belonged unto Herod's jurisdiction, he sent him to Herod, who himself also was at Jerusalem at that time.	e. The attempt by Pilate to escape his duty
1. The setting: The Sanhedrin dragged Jesus before Pilate[DS1]	And the whole multitude of them arose, and led him unto Pilate.	8 And when Herod saw Jesus, he was exceeding glad: for he was desirous to see him of a long season, because he had heard many things of	**3. The questioning before Herod: Shirking concern** a. He sought the spectacular

2. The trial before Pilate: Shirking duty
a. The charges against Jesus[DS2]
  1) He is a revolutionary
  2) He opposes taxes
  3) He claims to be a King
b. The questioning of Pilate & the claim of Jesus
	2 And they began to accuse him, saying, We found this fellow perverting the nation, and forbidding to give tribute to Caesar, saying that himself is Christ a King.
	3 And Pilate asked him, saying, Art thou the King of the Jews? And he answered and said, Thou sayest it.
		him; and he hoped to have seen some miracle done by him.
		9 Then he questioned with him in many words; but he answered him nothing.
		10 And the chief priests and scribes stood and vehemently accused him.
			b. He was the only man Jesus never answered
			
			c. He listened to false charges by the religionists

c. The verdict by Pilate: Jesus was innocent d. The bitter protest & enlarged charge of the crowd	4 Then said Pilate to the chief priests and to the people, I find no fault in this man. 5 And they were the more fierce, saying, He stirreth up the people, teaching throughout all Jewry, beginning from Galilee to this place.	11 And Herod with his men of war set him at nought, and mocked him, and arrayed him in a gorgeous robe, and sent him again to Pilate. 12 And the same day Pilate and Herod were made friends together: for before they were at enmity between themselves.	d. He did not take Jesus seriously: Ridiculed & mocked Him—contemptuously **4. The conclusion: Pilate & Herod were brought together in their opposition to Jesus**

DIVISION XI

THE SON OF MAN'S SUFFERINGS: HIS AGONY, TRIALS, AND CRUCIFIXION, 22:39–23:56

E. Jesus' First Trial Before Pilate and Herod: The Shirking of Duty and Personal Concern, 23:1-12

(23:1-12) **Introduction**: this passage is a clear portrait of two men who shirked duty and personal concern.
1. The setting: the Sanhedrin dragged Jesus before Pilate (v.1).
2. The trial before Pilate: shirking duty (vv.2-7).
3. The questioning before Herod: shirking concern (vv.8-11).
4. The conclusion: Pilate and Herod were brought together in their opposition to Jesus (v.12).

1 (23:1) **Religionists**: the Sanhedrin dragged Jesus before Pilate. Feelings ran deep. The depth of their obstinate unbelief is seen in the fact that "the *whole multitude* of them arose and led Him to Pilate." Just picture the scene. All members present (seventy one when a full body was present) marched Him to Pilate. They were so opposed to Him that they wanted the full weight of their position and their comrades standing against Him.

> **Thought 1.** Observe obstinate unbelievers. They try to convince and secure as much support as possible against Christ and His followers. Why? To protect their worldly desires and security, their position and authority and wealth.

DEEPER STUDY # 1
(23:1-7) **Pilate**: see DEEPER STUDY # 1—Lu.23:13.

2 (23:2-7) **Jesus Christ, Trials—Pilate**: the trial before Pilate is a clear picture of *shirking duty*. Note five points.
1. The political charges against Jesus were three (see DEEPER STUDY # 2—Lu.23:2).
2. The questioning of Pilate and the claim of Jesus. This was one of the charges brought against Jesus, and in the eyes of Rome it would be the most serious. Pilate, somewhat surprised by the charge, scornfully asked Jesus, "Art thou the King of the Jews?" Jesus strongly claimed that He was: "Thou sayest it." However, as John points out, Jesus clearly stated that His kingdom was not of this world. His kingdom was spiritual (Jn.18:36-37).

14

Thought 1. Jesus is not a political revolutionary, not a threat to any civil government. He is the King of man's spirit and of heaven, of the spiritual dimension of being, not of earth. He came to rule and reign in the hearts and lives of men, in the realm of the spiritual and eternal, not in the realm of the physical and temporal (see note—Ep.1:3).

3. The verdict of Pilate: Jesus was innocent. Note: this is a public verdict. Pilate actually pronounced Jesus innocent to the leaders and the people. However, as shall be seen and as is the case with so many, he lacked the *inner strength* to stand by his convictions. He gave in to the world, going along with their wish.

4. The bitter protest and enlarged charge. The unbelievers, fitfully aroused, accused Jesus. They were closeminded: obstinate, bitter, spiteful. They said He was guilty of leading a revolution throughout all Israel, from Galilee to Jerusalem.

It should be noted that Jesus' purpose was not to defend Himself nor to escape death. His purpose was to surrender to the *sinful behavior* of men. The *sinful behavior* to which He submitted was...

- the very depth of sin itself
- the ultimate demonstration of sin
- the greatest sin that could be committed

The act of sin to which He subjected Himself was the rejection and killing of the Son of God. Standing there before His accusers, He said nothing, enduring their awful indignities. He endured because He was purposed to die for the sins of men.

Note that Pilate actually declared Jesus innocent four different times (Lu.23:4, 14, 15, 22; see Jn.18:38; 19:4, 6).

5. The attempt to escape one's duty (Pilate). Pilate wished to release Jesus, for he knew the Lord was innocent. However, he had to guard against upsetting the leaders of the Jewish nation. He was in a dilemma. When he heard Galilee mentioned, he saw a way out of his dilemma. Herod, who was ruler of Galilee, was in town for the Passover. He could send Jesus over to Herod and let him pass judgment. As a Galilaean, Jesus belonged under the jurisdiction of Herod.

The point to note is this: Pilate lacked the courage to do what was right. He knew Jesus was innocent, yet he sought to *escape his duty* to declare the truth. He made four attempts to shirk his duty. (1) He tried to get the Jews to handle the matter themselves (Lu.18:31). (2) He sent Jesus to Herod (Lu.23:7). (3) He tried to get the Jews to accept Jesus as the prisoner to be released at the Passover (Lu.23:17-19; Mk.15:6). (4) He suggested flogging Jesus and then letting Him go (Lu.23:16).

Thought 1. A man who seeks to escape his duty is an unworthy leader. He is not worthy of the responsibility (position, call, or duty).

"**A double minded man is unstable in all his ways**" (Js.1:8).
"**Draw nigh to God, and he will draw nigh to you. Cleanse your hands, ye sinners; and purify your hearts, ye double minded**" (Js.4:8).
"**No servant can serve two masters: for either he will hate the one, and love the other; or else he will hold to the one, and despise the other. Ye cannot serve God and mammon**" (Lu.16:13).
"**Their heart is divided; now shall they be found faulty**" (Ho.10:2).

DEEPER STUDY # 2
(23:2) **Jesus Christ, Charges Against**: three political charges were leveled against Jesus.

1. He was charged with perverting the nation, that is, of treason, of being a revolutionary and committing sedition against Rome. The charge, of course, was false. Jesus was not out to pervert people from an earthly nation; He was out to convert people to a heavenly world, to God and His kingdom which were not of this earth (Jn.19:36).

2. He was charged with disobeying the laws of the nation, in particular for not paying taxes. Of course this charge was also false. Jesus had taught that obedience to earthly government was absolutely essential for the believer. (See outline and notes—Lu.20:19-26.)

3. He was charged with claiming to be King, with being a rival to Caesar. Again, this charge was false.
   a. The very reason the Jewish leaders were not accepting Him (so they claimed) was because He had come in the meekness and love of God, not in the armed might of God, liberating their nation from the Roman conquerors (see DEEPER STUDY # 2—Mt.1:18).
   b. Jesus had actually refused to let the people set Him up as King (Jn.6:15).

---

3 (23:8-11) **Herod's Hardened Heart**: the questioning before Herod is a clear picture of shirking personal concern.

Herod showed no concern whatsoever for the truth, nor for his own soul. The possibility that the true Messiah might actually be standing before Him never crossed his mind. (See note, pt.3—Lu.3:1. Also see DEEPER STUDY # 1,2, *Herod*—Mt.14:1-14 for more discussion.)

1. Herod sought only the spectacular. He had heard many things about Jesus, the amazing power and miracles He had manifested. As a ruler, a very special person, Herod wanted and felt he deserved...

- the privilege of some sign
- the privilege of gazing
- the privilege of some spectacle

Jesus' power, of course, was not to be used for the spectacular, not for the purpose of satisfying an unbeliever's curiosity. (See notes—Lu.4:9-12; 11:20 for more discussion.)

2. Herod was the only man Jesus never answered. Herod's own household had been penetrated with the gospel. Chuza, Herod's personal steward (Lu.8:3), and Manaen, Herod's foster brother (Ac.13:1), were believers. The nobleman or court official mentioned in the story shared by Jesus was also probably of Herod's court (Jn.4:46). Apparently, the gospel as lived by these persons had little effect upon Herod. Their sharing was but religious foolishness to him. He treated their reports with disdain, perhaps with some abuse. Jesus, knowing the hopelessness of his unresponsive heart, wasted no time and no words upon him. Jesus said nothing to him at all.

3. Herod listened to false charges by the religionists. He had failed to listen to John the Baptist (Lu.9:7-9) and to the witnesses in his own household. He had heard "many things of Christ" (v.8), yet he had refused to listen, to truly hear and heed. But now, with Jesus standing before him, he listened to the false charges of those who opposed Jesus.

4. Herod set Jesus at nought, treated Him as unimportant. The word *nought* (exouthenesas) means to count as nothing, to make nothing of, to think something is unimportant, to count as zero—therefore, to treat with utter contempt.

Note the contrast in the verse. Herod sat there as King "with his men of war" surrounding him, and Jesus stood there beaten and battered in torn, ragged clothes. Herod, judging by appearance, counted the Man who claimed to be the Son of God as nothing. This Man and His claim did not matter, not to Herod.

> **Thought 1.** Many count Christ as unimportant. They think He does not matter—that He can be excluded from life, that He and His claim are meaningless. Such people go about counting their own lives and worldly ways dear unto themselves. (See Lu.9:24; 17:33.)
>
> > "Whosoever shall seek to save his life shall lose it; and whosoever shall lose his life shall preserve it" (Lu.17:33).
> >
> > "And take heed to yourselves, lest at any time your hearts be overcharged with surfeiting, and drunkenness, and cares of this life, and so that day come upon you unawares" (Lu.21:34).
> >
> > "He that believeth on the Son hath everlasting life: and he that believeth not the Son shall not see life; but the wrath of God abideth on him" (Jn.3:36).
> >
> > "I said therefore unto you, that ye shall die in your sins: for if ye believe not that I am he, ye shall die in your sins" (Jn.8:24).
> >
> > "Take heed, brethren, lest there be in any of you an evil heart of unbelief, in departing from the living God" (He.3:12).

4 (23:12) **World, Rejection of Jesus**: Pilate and Herod became friends. They had formerly been enemies. But when confronted by the claims of Christ, they united together in order to oppose Christ. The worldly are often brought together in their opposition to Christ.

> "The world cannot hate you; but me it hateth, because I testify of it, that the works thereof are evil" (Jn.7:7).
>
> "If the world hate you, ye know that *it hated* me before it hated you. If ye were of the world, the world would love his own: but because ye are not of the world, but I have chosen you out of the world, therefore the world hateth you. Remember the word that I said unto you, The servant is not greater than his lord. If they have persecuted me, they will also persecute you; if they have kept my saying, they will keep yours also. But all these things will they do unto you for my name's sake, because they know not him that sent me. If I had not come and spoken unto them, they had not had sin: but now they have no cloke for their sin. He that hateth me hateth my Father also" (Jn.15:18-23).
>
> "But *this cometh to pass*, that the word might be fulfilled that is written in their law, They hated me without a cause" (Jn.15:25).

	F. Jesus' Second Trial Before Pilate: The Tragedy of a Compromising Man, 23:13-25 *(Mt. 27:15-25; Mk. 15:6-15; Jn. 18:39—19:16)*	man, and release unto us Barabbas. 19 (Who for a certain sedition made in the city, and for murder, was cast into prison.) 20 Pilate therefore, willing to release Jesus, spake again to them.	
1. Pilate tried selfishly to protect himself[DS1]	13 And Pilate, when he had called together the chief priests and the rulers and the people,		**3. Pilate gave in to worldly pressure**
a. A man who knew the truth	14 Said unto them, Ye have brought this man unto me, as one that perverteth the people: and, behold, I, having examined him before you, have found no fault in this man touching those things whereof ye accuse him: 15 No, nor yet Herod: for I sent you to him; and, lo, nothing worthy of death is done unto him.	21 But they cried, saying, Crucify him, crucify him. 22 And he said unto them the third time, Why, what evil hath he done? I have found no cause of death in him: I will therefore chastise him, and let him go.	a. He knew the truth: Jesus was innocent b. He faced loud voices against Jesus
b. A man who tried to appease others out of fear **2. Pilate tried to compromise truth & clear evidence**	16 I will therefore chastise him, and release him. 17 (For of necessity he must release one unto them at the feast.) 18 And they cried out all at once, saying, Away with this	23 And they were instant with loud voices, requiring that he might be crucified. And the voices of them and of the chief priests prevailed. 24 And Pilate gave sentence that it should be as they required. 25 And he released unto them him that for sedition and murder was cast into prison, whom they had desired; but he delivered Jesus to their will.	c. He compromised: Gave in to the worldly cries d. He allowed injustice, wrong, & evil to be done

DIVISION XI

THE SON OF MAN'S SUFFERINGS: HIS AGONY, TRIALS, AND CRUCIFIXION, 22:39–23:56

F. Jesus' Second Trial Before Pilate: The Tragedy of a Compromising Man, 23:13-25

(23:13-25) **Introduction**: compromising with the world is sin. Compromise always leads to trouble and tragedy. Pilate is the picture of a man whose compromise led to the greatest tragedy in human history.
1. Pilate tried selfishly to protect himself (vv.13-16).
2. Pilate tried to compromise truth and clear evidence (vv.17-21).
3. Pilate gave in to worldly pressure (vv.22-25).

[1] (23:13-16) **Compromise—Appeasement—Injustice**: Pilate tried selfishly to protect himself. He called the court back into session. A decision had been made; he was now ready to give his verdict.
  ⇒ He had examined Jesus and found no fault in Him: Jesus was innocent.
  ⇒ He had sent Jesus to Herod for a verdict, and Herod found Jesus innocent.
  ⇒ No crime worthy of death had been committed by Jesus. Pilate had decided, therefore, that he would chastise Jesus and release Him.

Note that Pilate was trying to appease the Jews. He knew the truth: Jesus was innocent. Jesus should be released and the Jews' behavior rebuked, but Pilate feared displeasing and inflaming the Jews. He was afraid they might cause trouble for him, reporting him to Rome and causing him to lose his position and rule (see DEEPER STUDY # 1—Lu.23:13). Throughout the whole scene Pilate's primary interest was himself, not truth and justice.

  Thought 1. A compromising man is self-centered. He seeks to protect himself even at the expense of the truth and justice. He fears losing...
  • position   • security
  • power   • image
  • influence   • acceptance
  • job   • friends

  "Ye shall do no unrighteousness in judgment; thou shalt not respect the person of the poor, nor honour the person of the mighty: but in righteousness shalt thou judge thy neighbour" (Le.19:15).
  "How long will ye judge unjustly, and accept the persons of the wicked?" (Ps.82:2).

"And moreover I saw under the sun the place of judgment, that wickedness was there; and the place of righteousness, that iniquity was there" (Ec.3:16).

"Therefore have I also made you contemptible and base before all the people, according as ye have not kept my ways, but have been partial in the law" (Mal.2:9).

"I charge thee before God, and the Lord Jesus Christ, and the elect angels, that thou observe these things without preferring one before another, doing nothing by partiality" (1 Ti.5:21).

"I call heaven and earth to record this day against you, that I have set before you life and death, blessing and cursing: therefore choose life, that both thou and thy seed may live" (De.30:19).

DEEPER STUDY # 1

(23:13) **Pilate**: the procurator of Judea. He was directly responsible to the Emperor for the administrative and financial management of the country. A man had to work himself up through the political and military ranks to become a procurator. Pilate was, therefore, an able man, experienced in the affairs of politics and government as well as the military. He held office for ten years which shows that he was highly trusted by the Roman government. However, the Jews despised Pilate, and Pilate despised the Jews for their intense practice of religion. When Pilate became procurator of Judea, he did two things that aroused the people's bitter hatred against him forever. First, on his state visits to Jerusalem, he and his military guard rode their stallions into the city with the Roman standard, an eagle sitting atop a pole. All previous governors had removed the standard because of the Jews' opposition to idols. Second, Pilate launched the construction of a new water supply for Jerusalem. To finance the project, he took the money out of the temple treasury. The Jews never forgot or forgave this act. They bitterly opposed Pilate all through his reign, and he treated them with equal contempt (see DEEPER STUDY # 1—Mk.15:1-15). On several occasions, Jewish leaders threatened to exercise their right to report Pilate to the emperor. This, of course, disturbed Pilate to no end and caused him to become even more bitter and contemptuous toward the Jews.

---

2 (23:17-21) **Compromise**: Pilate tried to compromise the truth despite clear evidence. He saw the evidence: Jesus was innocent, and the religionists were only envious of Jesus, feeling He was a threat to their security. Pilate wanted to declare Jesus innocent, but he felt he had to satisfy the cries of these religious worldlings as well. Therefore, he conceived a compromise. It was a long time custom for Rome to release a popular prisoner to the Jews at the Passover Feast in order to humor and secure more cooperation from the population. Within the prison was a notorious criminal, Barabbas. Pilate had him brought before the people along with Jesus and shouted out that the people could choose which one was to be released.

Pilate felt sure that by pitting Barabbas against Jesus, the people would choose Jesus, the One who had ministered and helped so many of them. How wrong the man of compromise was. (The world will always cry out against Jesus to get rid of Him.)

The point to note is the moral weakness of Pilate. He knew Jesus was innocent. He knew the Jews sought to kill Jesus because they envied Him. Jesus should have been released immediately, but Pilate attempted a compromise instead of standing up for the truth.

Thought 1. Note a crucial point: when the truth is known, it should be proclaimed, not compromised. Com-promise results in three tragedies.
1) Compromise weakens character and testimony.
2) Compromise means that the truth is not being done or lived. A person is agreeing to do something less than what he should be doing.
3) Compromise weakens principle, position, and life.

Thought 2. God accepts no compromise concerning His Son, Jesus Christ. A man either stands for Christ or against Christ. There is no neutral ground. Christ is innocent and sinless; He is the Ideal Man, the Son of God in whom all men are to place their trust.

"He that is not with me is against me: and he that gathereth not with me scattereth" (Lu.11:23).

"All men should honour the Son, even as they honour the Father. He that honoureth not the Son honoureth not the Father which hath sent him. Verily, verily, I say unto you, He that heareth my word, and believeth on him that sent me, hath everlasting life, and shall not come into condemnation; but is passed from death unto life" (Jn.5:23-24).

"And this is the record, that God hath given to us eternal life, and this life is in his Son. He that hath the Son hath life; and he that hath not the Son of God hath not life" (1 Jn.5:11-12).

"Submit yourselves therefore to God. Resist the devil, and he will flee from you. Draw nigh to God, and he will draw nigh to you. Cleanse your hands, ye sinners; and purify your hearts, ye double minded. Be afflicted, and mourn, and weep: let your laughter be turned to mourning, and your joy to heaviness. Humble yourselves in the sight of the Lord, and he shall lift you up" (Js.4:7-10).

3 (23:22-25) **Worldliness—Compromise**: Pilate gave in to worldly pressure. The scene was dramatic, but tragic. The scene can be simply stated. Pilate...
- knew Jesus was innocent (v.22)
- faced loud voices against Jesus (v.23)
- compromised and gave in to the worldly cries (v.24)
- allowed injustice and wrong and sin to be done (v.25)

The point is this: Pilate, the compromising man, was *morally weak*.

⇒ He was not strong enough to do what he knew was right.
⇒ He lacked the moral strength to stand up for Jesus.
⇒ He was too weak to declare the truth.

Thought 1. The pressure of the world to do evil is great. Indecision and compromise are not the way to face the world: decisive dedication to Christ and separation from the world alone can conquer the world.

"I beseech you therefore, brethren, by the mercies of God, that ye present your bodies a living sacrifice, holy, acceptable unto God, which is your reasonable service. And be not conformed to this world: but be ye transformed by the renewing of your mind, that ye may prove what is that good, and acceptable, and perfect, will unto God" (Ro.12:1-2).

"Wherefore come out from among them, and be ye separate, saith the Lord, and touch not the unclean thing; and I will receive you, and will be a Father unto you, and ye shall be my sons and daughters, saith the Lord Almighty" (2 Co.6:17-18).

"Love not the world, neither the things that are in the world. If any man love the world, the love of the Father is not in him. For all that is in the world, the lust of the flesh, and the lust of the eyes, and the pride of life, is not of the Father, but is of the world" (1 Jn.2:15-16).

Thought 2. Most men prefer the company of evil, sinful men to that of the Prince of Life. Note: even worldly religionists choose the world over the Prince of Life.

Thought 3. Note a crucial point. It is when we are indecisive or willing to compromise that the pressure to do evil gets to us. Hesitating and being indecisive will cause us to give in to the pressure of sin.

"By faith Moses, when he was come to years, refused to be called the son of Pharaoh's daughter; choosing rather to suffer affliction with the people of God, than to enjoy the pleasures of sin for a season" (He.11:24-25).

"Ye therefore, beloved, seeing ye know these things before, beware lest ye also, being led away with the error of the wicked, fall from your own stedfastness" (2 Pe.3:17).

1. The man who bore His cross: A picture of conversion	**G. Jesus' Crucifixion & Its Events,**[DS1] **23:26-49** *(Mt. 27:26-56; Mk. 15:16-41; Jn. 19:16-37)* 26 And as they led him away, they laid hold upon one Simon, A Cyrenian, coming out of the country, and on him they laid the cross, that he might bear it after Jesus.	mocked him, coming to him, and offering him vinegar, 37 And saying, If thou be the king of the Jews, save thyself. 38 And a superscription also was written over him in letters of Greek, and Latin, and Hebrew, THIS IS THE KING OF THE JEWS.	soldiers 1) Offering Him vinegar-wine[DS2] 2) His claim to be King **9. The inscription on the cross: A misunderstood charge**
2. The great crowd of mourners: A picture of hearts that felt for Jesus	27 And there followed him a great company of people, and of women, which also bewailed and lamented him.	39 And one of the malefactors which were hanged railed on him, saying, If thou be Christ, save thyself and us.	**10. The unrepentant thief: A picture of hardness even in death**
3. The prediction of Jerusalem's doom: A picture of coming judgment a. So terrible, people should weep over b. So terrible, people will wish to be childless	28 But Jesus turning unto them said, Daughters of Jerusalem, weep not for me, but weep for yourselves, and for your children. 29 For, behold, the days are coming, in the which they shall say, Blessed are the barren, and the wombs that never bare, and the paps which never gave suck.	40 But the other answering rebuked him, saying, Dost not thou fear God, seeing thou art in the same condemnation? 41 And we indeed justly; for we receive the due reward of our deeds: but this man hath done nothing amiss. 42 And he said unto Jesus, Lord, remember me when thou comest into thy kingdom.	**11. The repentant thief: A picture of true repentance** a. Feared God b. Declared Jesus' righteousness c. Asked Jesus for a place in His kingdom
c. So terrible, people will wish to be buried alive d. So terrible because judgment is inevitable	30 Then shall they begin to say to the mountains, Fall on us; and to the hills, Cover us. 31 For if they do these things in a green tree, what shall be done in the dry?	43 And Jesus said unto him, Verily I say unto thee, To day shalt thou be with me in paradise. 44 And it was about the sixth hour, and there was a darkness over all the earth until the ninth hour.	**12. The awesome darkness: A symbol of separation & loneliness**
4. The identification with criminals: Being numbered with sinners **5. The crucifixion: The summit of sin & love** a. At Mount Calvary b. Crucified between two criminals	32 And there were also two other, malefactors, led with him to be put to death. 33 And when they were come to the place, which is called Calvary, there they crucified him, and the malefactors, one on the right hand, and the other on the left.	45 And the sun was darkened, and the veil of the temple was rent in the midst. 46 And when Jesus had cried with a loud voice, He said, Father, into thy hands I commend my spirit: and having said thus, he gave up the ghost.	**13. The torn veil of the temple: A symbol of open access into God's presence** **14. The great cry of trust: A picture of glorious triumph**
6. The prayer for His enemies: Forgiveness **7. The gambling for His clothes: Being stripped by greed** **8. The mocking: Misunderstanding His salvation** a. Misunderstood by the people & religionists 1) His claim to save 2) His claim to be Messiah b. Misunderstood by the	34 Then said Jesus, Father, forgive them; for they know not what they do. And they parted his raiment, and cast lots. 35 And the people stood beholding. And the rulers also with them derided him, saying, He saved others; let him save himself, if he be Christ, the chosen of God. 36 And the soldiers also	47 Now when the centurion saw what was done, he glorified God, saying, Certainly this was a righteous man. 48 And all the people that came together to that sight, beholding the things which were done, smote their breasts, and returned. 49 And all his acquaintance, and the women that followed him from Galilee, stood afar off, beholding these things.	**15. The centurion's declaration: Jesus' righteousness—a confession to be made by many** **16. The people's grief: A picture of stricken conscience** **17. The followers of Jesus: A proof that Jesus lived & served well**

DIVISION XI

THE SON OF MAN'S SUFFERINGS: HIS AGONY, TRIALS, AND CRUCIFIXION, 22:39–23:56

G. Jesus' Crucifixion and Its Events, 23:26-49

(23:26-49) **Introduction:** the crucifixion of Jesus Christ is both the most shocking event and the most wonderful event of human history. It is the most shocking event in that it is the creature murdering the Creator. It is the most wonderful event in that it is the Creator saving the creature. (Glance at the outline above for the *seventeen events* of the crucifixion as covered by *Luke*.)

DEEPER STUDY # 1
(23:26-49) **Crucifixion, The**: see outline, note, and DEEPER STUDY # 1—Mt.27:26-44 for more discussion.

---

1 (23:26) **Conversion—Simon of Cyrene**: there was the man who bore Jesus' cross—a picture of conversion. Note several things.

1. God's plan or providence. Nothing happens by chance, not to the Christian believer. God oversees the life of His people. Thus, Simon's being pressed into carrying the cross for Jesus was in the plan of God.

2. Simon was apparently a pilgrim coming to celebrate the Passover. He was standing along the roadway watching the armed procession make its way through the streets. Apparently there was some expression of concern and sympathy for Jesus, something within his heart that was touched and that reached out to Jesus. God knew this, and directed the soldiers to enlist his help in carrying the Lord's cross.

3. Simon was "the father of Alexander and Rufus" (Mk.15:21). The comment by Mark is interesting. Evidently they were known believers (see Ac.13:1; Ro.16:13). The indication is that Simon or at least his two sons were eventually converted.

Thought 1. The man who takes up the cross of Christ will be converted.

> "And he said to them all, If any man will come after me, let him deny himself, and take up his cross daily, and follow me" (Lu.9:23).

2 (23:27) **Godly Sorrow—Sympathy**: there was the great crowd of mourners—a picture of hearts that felt for Jesus. A great crowd of people followed and felt for Jesus, especially women. The word *bewailed* (ekoptonto) means to cut, strike, smite, beat. They were cut to the core of their hearts, actually feeling pain for Jesus. The word *lamented* (ethrenoun) means to cry out loud, to mourn, groan. They were crying out, unable to hold back the pain cutting their hearts. Some of the people, of course, had been followers of Jesus for a long time and were feeling the depth of their Lord's sufferings; whereas other onlookers, as in any crowd witnessing severe suffering, felt only a natural tenderness and lament over one's suffering so much.

Thought 1. A natural response to the Lord's sufferings is not enough. A person must *understand* why Christ suffered and must feel a *godly sorrow* over Christ's having to bear the sins of the world (see DEEPER STUDY # 1—2 Co.7:10).

> "For godly sorrow worketh repentance to salvation not to be repented of: but the sorrow of the world worketh death" (2 Co.7:10).
> "Remember them that are in bonds, as bound with them; and them which suffer adversity, as being yourselves also in the body" (He.13:3).

3 (23:28-31) **Jerusalem, Prophecy of**: there was the prediction of Jerusalem's doom—a picture of coming judgment. The significant point to note is what was upon Jesus' mind: judgment. The people had rejected God's Messiah and salvation, choosing to go the way of the world, and the way of the world was doom and destruction. The destruction coming would be so terrible, people...

- would weep for themselves
- would wish to be childless
- would wish to be buried alive

Verse 31 is a proverbial saying: if the world (Rome) treats a green tree like this (Him, a tree with its full provision of sap), how will it treat a dry tree like Israel, a tree with little if any provision of sap, a tree of no use, with no life left, ready to be cut down and destroyed?

Thought 1. Jerusalem rejected the invitation of God time and again. However, God was patient and demonstrated His patience for generations, but the rejection and killing of His Son were too great to leave unpunished. As soon as Christianity could get a solid foothold in the world, Jerusalem was to be judged and doomed. (See outline and notes—Lu.20:13-18.)

God is patient with every man. But continued rejection of His Son brings judgment and eternal doom.

> "For God so loved the world, that he gave his only begotten Son, that whosoever believeth in him should not perish, but have everlasting life. For God sent not his Son into the world to condemn the world; but that the world through him might be saved. He that believeth on him is not condemned: but he that believeth not is condemned already, because he hath not believed in the name of the only begotten Son of God" (Jn.3:16-18).
> "And as it is appointed unto men once to die, but after this the judgment" (He.9:27).

4 (23:32) **Jesus Christ, Identified with Sinners**: there was the identification with criminals—a picture of being numbered with sinners. Why was Jesus crucified with criminals? Scripture does not say, but perhaps this was a day set aside for execution, or perhaps the Jewish leaders pressed Pilate to execute Jesus with other criminals. By this, they hoped to add weight to their position that He was no more than a mere man, an imposter who deserved to die just as other criminals. Whatever the reason, the fact that the Son of God was executed right along with other criminals adds to the shame and reproach He bore. This event had been prophesied just as many others had (Is.53:12).

Thought 1. Christ was counted as a sinner that He might bear the sin of many.

"**He was numbered with the transgressors; and he bare the sin of many, and made intercession for the transgressors**" (**Is.53:12**).

5 (23:33) **Crucifixion, The**: the crucifixion was the summit of both sin and love. It was the summit of sin in that Jesus bore the sins of all humanity for all time. He even became "sin for us," the very embodiment of sin (2 Co.5:21; 1 Pe.2:24). It was the summit of love in that God willingly gave up His only Son to die on the cross for the sins of all humanity. And Christ voluntarily surrendered Himself to bear the sins of the world. What greater love could ever be demonstrated to the human race? The crucifixion was the most horrible death imaginable. There was the pain of the spikes being driven through the flesh of Jesus' hands and feet or ankles. There was the weight of His body jolting and pulling against the spikes as the cross was lifted and rocked into place. There was the scorching sun and the unquenchable thirst gnawing away at His dry mouth and throat. There was the blood oozing from His scourged back, His thorn-crowned brow, and His stick-beaten head. In addition, imagine the aggravation of flies, gnats, and other insects buzzing about and landing on His bleeding face. Moreover, for Jesus, there was the piercing pain of the spear thrust into His side. On and on the sufferings could be described. There has never been a more cruel form of execution than crucifixion upon a cross.

The crucifixion took place on a hill called *the skull* (in Latin, calvaria). We get the name Calvary from the Latin word. (See note, pt.11—Mt.27:26-38.)

Thought 1. In the simplest of terms, Christ was crucified for our sins in order to bring us to God.

"**Who his own self bare our sins in his own body on the tree, that we, being dead to sins, should live unto righteousness: by whose stripes ye were healed**" (**1 Pe.2:24**).
"**For Christ also hath once suffered for sins, the just for the unjust, that he might bring us to God, being put to death in the flesh, but quickened by the Spirit**" (**1 Pe.3:18**).

Note that two criminals were crucified with Him. He was dying because of them and because of all other men. Why? Because all men are criminals against God, rebelling against Him and breaking His commandments.

"**For all have sinned, and come short of the glory of God**" (**Ro.3:23**).
"**This is a faithful saying, and worthy of all acceptation, that Christ Jesus came into the world to save sinners; of whom I am chief**" (**1 Ti.1:15**).
"**For Christ also hath once suffered for sins, the just for the unjust, that he might bring us to God, being put to death in the flesh, but quickened by the Spirit**" (**1 Pe.3:18**).

6 (23:34) **Forgiveness—Salvation**: there was the prayer for His enemies—a picture of love and forgiveness to the end. The picture is of Jesus the Mediator. He had come for this very purpose, to stand as the Mediator between God and sinful man. Therefore upon the cross, He prayed for those who stood below crucifying Him. Note several things.
1. It had been predicted that Christ would pray for transgressors (Is.53:12).
2. He prayed for God to forgive those who were crucifying Him. The very purpose for His coming was to make provision for forgiveness of sins. Because of His death, God would be able to forgive the sins of men, even those who were now crucifying Him.
3. The men crucifying Him did not know what they were doing. They did not know who He was.

"**None of the princes of this world knew: for had they known it, they would not have crucified the Lord of glory**" (**1 Co.2:8**).

Thought 1. The most wonderful truth in all the world is this: God will hold no sin against any man if that man will personally trust His Son. If God forgives the men who killed His only Son, God will forgive any man for any sin—if that man will just ask.

"**The God of our fathers raised up Jesus, whom ye slew and hanged on a tree. Him hath God exalted with his right hand to be a Prince and a Saviour, for to give repentance to Israel, and forgiveness of sins**" (**Ac.5:30-31**).
"**Repent therefore of this thy wickedness, and pray God, if perhaps the thought of thine heart may be forgiven thee**" (**Ac.8:22**).
"**Be it known unto you therefore, men and brethren, that through this man is preached unto you the forgiveness of sins: and by him all that believe are justified from all things, from which ye could not be justified by the law of Moses**" (**Ac.13:38-39**).
"**In whom we have redemption through his blood, even the forgiveness of sins**" (**Col.1:14; see Col.2:13**).

7 (23:34) **Mortality—Immortality**: there was the gambling for His clothes—a picture of being stripped by the selfishness, greed, and sin of men. Note two points.

1. The custom seems to have been for the executing soldiers to claim whatever they wished of the clothes of crucified criminals. The soldiers stripped Jesus, dividing His clothes among themselves. However, His coat was valuable: it was seamless, one piece of cloth, woven from top to bottom just as the High Priest's coat or cloak was. The soldiers, therefore, decided to gamble by casting lots for it (Jn.19:23-24). This event was foretold in Ps.22:18.

2. Jesus was stripped by the soldiers, stripped of His mortal clothes. There is symbolism in this act: He allowed all His mortality to be stripped so that He might abolish death and bring life and immortality to light.

> "But [God's grace] is now made manifest by the appearing of our Savior Jesus Christ, who hath abolished death, and hath brought life and immortality to light through the gospel" (2 Ti.1:10).

8 (23:35-37) **Salvation**: there was the mockery, the misunderstanding of His salvation. Note those who mocked and taunted Him.

1. The people and religionists mocked His claim to be the Savior and Messiah. They totally misunderstood God's Messiahship. Both the people and the religionists should have been above this kind of behavior. In addition, they had every opportunity to believe, for He had not hid Himself or His message of salvation. But being part of a sinful crowd and their own unbelief, they led each other to do shameful things.

> "...Christ [Messiah] Jesus who gave himself a ransom for all, to be testified in due time" (1 Ti.2:5-6).
> "This is a faithful saying, and worthy of all acceptation, that Christ [Messiah] Jesus came into the world to save sinners" (1 Ti.1:15).

Thought 1. Leaders, civil and religious, are still men. It is not the position or profession that makes a man, but the heart. A heart of unbelief and enmity, a heart willing to become a participant with the sinful crowd, will stoop to do shameful things, no matter the position or profession.

> "Behold, your house is left unto you desolate" (Mt.23:38).

2. The soldiers mocked and taunted Him. In particular they mocked His claim to be King, but they did not understand His claim (Jn.18:36. See Jn.18:33-37; Mt.27:11.)

DEEPER STUDY # 2

(23:36) **Vinegar**: Jesus was offered drugged wine at the beginning of the crucifixion, but He refused it (Mt.27:34; Mk.15:23). He was also offered vinegar just before His death (Jn.19:29), and here the soldiers use vinegar in some form of mockery with Him.

---

9 (23:38) **Jesus Christ, King**: there was the inscription on the cross—a misunderstood charge. The sign placed above His head, "The King of the Jews," was intended to mock the Jewish authorities and to reproach His claim. However, God overruled and used the sign to proclaim the truth to the whole world (Lu.23:38). The very charges against Jesus proclaimed His deity and honor.

> "He humbled himself, and became obedient unto death, even the death of the cross. Wherefore God also hath highly exalted him, and given him a name which is above every name: that at the name of Jesus every knee should bow, of things in heaven, and things in earth, and things under the earth; and that every tongue should confess that Jesus Christ is Lord, to the glory of God the Father" (Ph.2:8-11).
> "Our Lord Jesus Christ: which in his times he shall show, who is the blessed and only Potentate, the King of kings, and Lord of lords; who only hath immortality, dwelling in the light which no man can approach unto; whom no man hath seen, nor can see: to whom be honour and power everlasting. Amen" (1 Ti.6:14-16).

10 (23:39) **Unbelief**: there was the unrepentant thief—a picture of hardness even in death. The thieves heard the crowd mock Jesus about being the Messiah, the Savior of the world. Hanging there as criminals, guilty before God and men, they should have been searching to see if there were any chance that Jesus could have been who He claimed. They needed to be saved and forgiven. One criminal showed enormous hardness of heart. He mocked the very thought that Jesus was the Christ.

> "For God so loved the world, that he gave his only begotten Son, that whosoever believeth in him should not perish, but have everlasting life. For God sent not his Son into the world to condemn the world; but that the world through him might be saved. He that believeth on Him is not condemned: but he that believeth not is condemned already, because he hath not believed in the name of the only begotten Son of God" (Jn.3:16-18).

11 (23:40-43) **Salvation—Repentance**: there was the repentant thief—a picture of true repentance. The second thief demonstrated the steps to salvation and true repentance.
⇒ He feared God (v.40).
⇒ He declared that Jesus was righteous (v.41).
⇒ He asked for Jesus to remember him (v.42).

Note that Jesus promised him eternal life; the repentant man was to be with Christ in paradise *that very day*. (See DEEPER STUDY # 3, *Paradise*—Lu.16:23.)

> **"Father, I will that they also, whom thou hast given me, be with me where I am; that they may behold my glory, which thou hast given me: for thou lovedst me before the foundation of the world" (Jn.17:24).**
> **"We are confident, I say, and willing rather to be absent from the body, and to be present with the Lord" (2 Co.5:8).**
> **"For I am in a strait betwixt two, having a desire to depart, and to be with Christ; which is far better" (Ph.1:23).**
> **"If any man serve me, let him follow me; and where I am, there shall also my servant be: if any man serve me, him will my Father honour" (Jn.12:26).**

12 (23:44) **Judgment—Man, State of**: there was the awesome darkness—a symbol of separation and loneliness. The darkness told man something (see note—Mt.27:45 for detailed discussion).
1. Man was separated from the light.

> **"And this is the condemnation, that light is come into the world, and men loved darkness rather than light, because their deeds were evil. For every one that doeth evil hateth the light, neither cometh to the light, lest his deeds should be reproved" (Jn.3:19-20).**

2. Man stood all alone. He could not see in the dark, not well. He was, so to speak, standing in the world all alone, responsible for his own behavior; and he must face God someday all alone to give an account for his behavior.

> **"And it is appointed unto men once to die, but after this the judgment" (He.9:27).**

13 (23:45) **Access—Jesus Christ, Blood**: there was the torn veil of the temple—a symbol of open access into the very presence of God. Note four facts.
1. The veil (curtain) which was torn was the *inner veil* (katapetasma), the curtain which separated the Holy of Holies from the Holy Place. There was another veil, an *outer curtain* (kalumma), which separated the Holy Place from the outer court of the temple.
The Holy of Holies was the most sacred part of the temple. It was the place where the very presence of God was symbolized as dwelling in a very, very special way. It was closed *forever* to everyone except the High Priest. Even he could enter the Holy of Holies only once a year, on the Day of Atonement (Ex.26:33).
2. At the very hour that Jesus died, the High Priest would be rolling back the outer curtain in order to expose the Holy Place to the people who had gathered to worship in the surrounding court. As he rolled back the outer curtain exposing the Holy Place for worship, both he and the worshippers would stand in amazement. Why? Because they would see the inner veil rent from the top to the bottom. There they would stand, experiencing and witnessing the Holy of Holies, the very special place where the presence of God Himself was supposed to dwell—a sight that the people had never seen before.
3. The veil was torn from top to bottom. This symbolized that it was torn by an act of God Himself. It symbolized God's giving direct access into His presence (He.6:19; 9:3-12, 24; 10:19-23). Now, through the body of Christ, any man can enter the presence of God anytime, anyplace.

> **"By the which will we are sanctified through the offering of the body of Jesus Christ once for all" (He.10:10).**

4. The torn veil symbolized that all men could now draw near God by the blood of Christ.

> **"But now in Christ Jesus ye who sometimes were far off are made nigh by the blood of Christ. For he is our peace, who hath made both one, and hath broken down the middle wall of partition between us" (Ep.2:13-14).**

14 (23:46) **Jesus Christ, Work—Purpose**: there was the great cry of trust—a picture of glorious triumph. What Jesus cried out was one word in the Greek, *Tetelestai*, "It is finished" (Jn.19:30). It was a cry of purpose, a shout of triumph. He was dying for a specific purpose and that purpose was now fulfilled (see note—Mt.27:50 for detailed discussion).

> **"I am the door: by me if any man enter in, he shall be saved, and shall go in and out, and find pasture....I am the good shepherd: the good shepherd giveth his life for the sheep....As the Father**

knoweth me, even so know I the Father: and I lay down my life for the sheep....Therefore doth my Father love me, because I lay down my life, that I might take it again. No man taketh it from me, but I lay it down of myself. I have power to lay it down, and I have power to take it again. This commandment have I received of my Father" (Jn.10:9, 11, 15, 17-18).

---

15 (23:47) **Confession**: there was the centurion's declaration—Jesus' righteousness, a picture of the confession to be made by many.

1. The centurion was bound to be a thoughtful and honest man. He was in charge of the crucifixion, which means he was responsible for overseeing all that took place. As the events unfolded upon the cross, he was stricken more and more with the claim of Jesus and the way in which the events were happening. When Jesus shouted out that His purpose was finished, that His death was the climax of His purpose upon earth, the centurion was convinced. The very fact that Jesus' death was purposeful was the clincher. God quickened to the soldier's heart the glorious truth: "Certainly this was a righteous man."

2. The centurion was a Gentile. He symbolized all who were to confess Christ in coming generations.

"That if thou shalt confess with thy mouth the Lord Jesus, and shalt believe in thine heart that God hath raised him from the dead, thou shalt be saved. For with the heart man believeth unto righteousness; and with the mouth confession is made unto salvation" (Ro.10:9-10).

---

16 (23:48) **Preparation—Conscience**: there was the people's grief—a picture of stricken consciences. The people had come for entertainment, but they went away with saddened, grieving hearts. God, being the Sovereign Lord of the universe, saw to it that they were stricken in conscience. They were being prepared for the preaching to come after Pentecost.

"How much more shall the blood of Christ, who through the eternal Spirit offered himself without spot to God, purge your conscience from dead works to serve the living God?" (He.9:14).

---

17 (23:49) **Self-Denial**: there were the followers of Jesus—a proof that Jesus lived and served well. Note that the women were at the cross despite the danger. They were off, some distance away, but they were there nevertheless. They still loved and cared, no matter what. They symbolized that Jesus' life was not in vain.

"For whosoever will save his life shall lose it; but whosoever shall lose his life for my sake and the gospel's, the same shall save it" (Mk.8:35).

	H. Jesus' Burial: Stirred to Step Forth for Jesus, 23:50-56 *(Mt. 27:57-61; Mk. 15:42-47; Jn. 19:38-42)*	Jesus. 53 And he took it down, and wrapped it in linen, and laid it in a sepulchre that was hewn in stone, wherein never man before was laid.	f. A man who cared deeply for Jesus 1) He took care of Jesus' body 2) He acted quickly
1. A secret believer stirred to step forward for Jesus a. A counselor b. A good & upright man c. A man who had feared to stand up for Jesus sometime before (Jn.19:38) d. A man who looked for the Messiah—for God's kingdom e. A man who was changed by the death of Jesus	50 And, behold, there was a man named Joseph, a counsellor; and he was a good man, and a just: 51 (The same had not consented to the counsel and deed of them;) he was of Arimathaea, a city of the Jews: who also himself waited for the kingdom of God. 52 This man went unto Pilate, and begged the body of	54 And that day was the preparation, and the sabbath drew on. 55 And the women also, which came with him from Galilee, followed after, and beheld the sepulchre, and how his body was laid. 56 And they returned, and prepared spices and ointments; and rested the sabbath day according to the commandment.	**2. The women stirred to loyalty & affection** a. Showed a fearless loyalty b. Showed deep affection c. Showed an ignorance of the resurrection

DIVISION XI

THE SON OF MAN'S SUFFERINGS: HIS AGONY, TRIALS, AND CRUCIFIXION, 22:39–23:56

H. Jesus' Burial: A Secret Disciple Stirred to Step Forth, 23:50-56

(23:50-56) **Introduction**: a secret believer is a tragedy. In a sense he is the tragedy of tragedies, for he fails to confess Jesus publicly. He ignores the fact of what Jesus said: all persons are lost (Mt.10:32-33). Joseph of Arimathaea was such a man: a secret believer until the death of Jesus. But the death of Jesus changed him.

1. The secret believer stirred to step forward for Jesus (vv.50-54).
2. The women stirred to loyalty and affection (vv.55-56).

1 (23:50-54) **Discipleship, Secret—Profession—Believer—Jesus Christ, Death**: the secret believer, Joseph of Arimathaea, was stirred to step forward for Jesus. A revealing description is given about Joseph.
1. He was a counselor, a senator, a member of the Sanhedrin, the ruling body of Israel. Apparently he was ...
   * highly educated
   * highly esteemed
   * well liked
   * very responsible
   * capable of leadership

2. He was a "good and just" man. He was a man...
   * of good quality
   * of high morals
   * of feelings
   * of compassion
   * of justice
   * of decision
   * of truth
   * of law

3. He was a man looking for the Messiah and the Kingdom of God (see notes—Lu.2:25-27; DEEPER STUDY # 3—Mt. 19:23-24).
4. He was, however, a man who feared to stand up for Jesus. John says he was "a disciple of Jesus, but secretly for fear of the Jews" (Jn.19:38). Joseph probably had met Jesus and arranged private meetings with Him when the Lord had visited Jerusalem, but he feared making a public profession. His position and prestige were at stake. His peers, the other rulers, opposed Jesus. He believed in Jesus, but out of fear he kept his discipleship a secret. Note: when the vote was taken to put Jesus to death, Joseph did abstain from voting, but he did not stand up for Jesus. He did not participate; he simply remained silent.

Thought 1. How many persons are like Joseph? They are believers and good and just people; however they fear what their friends and fellow workers will say. They fear the loss of position, prestige, promotion, acceptance, popularity, friends, job, income, livelihood.

"For whosoever shall be ashamed of me and of my words, of him shall the Son of man be ashamed, when he shall come in his own glory, and in his Father's, and of the holy angels" (Lu.9:26).
"And I say unto you my friends, Be not afraid of them that kill the body, and after that have no more that they can do. But I will forewarn you whom ye shall fear: Fear him, which after he hath killed hath power to cast into hell; yea, I say unto you, Fear not" (Lu.12:4-5).
"For God hath not given us the spirit of fear; but of power, and of love, and of a sound mind" (2 Ti.1:7).
"The fear of man bringeth a snare: but whoso putteth his trust in the LORD shall be safe" (Pr.29:25).

"I, even I, am he that comforteth you: who art thou, that thou shouldest be afraid of a man that shall die, and of the son of which shall be made as grass" (Is.51:12).

5. He was a man changed by the death of Jesus. This is seen in two facts.
   a. Joseph actually went to Pilate and begged for the body of Jesus. This was a tremendous act of courage. The Romans either dumped the bodies of crucified criminals in the trash heaps or left the bodies hanging upon the cross for the vultures and animals to consume. The latter served as an example of criminal punishment to the public. Joseph also braved the threat of Pilate's reaction. Pilate was fed up with the *Jesus matter*. Jesus had proven to be very bothersome to him. He could have reacted severely against Joseph.
   b. Joseph risked the disfavor and discipline of the Sanhedrin. They were the ruling body who had instigated and condemned Jesus, and Joseph was a member of the council. There was no question—he would face some harsh reaction from some of his fellow Sanhedrin members and from some of his closest friends.

The thing that turned Joseph from being a secret disciple to a bold disciple seems to be the cross, the phenomenal events surrounding the cross (the behavior and words of Jesus, the darkness, the earthquake, the torn veil, and other events). When Joseph witnessed all this, his mind connected the claims of Jesus with the Old Testament prophecies of the Messiah. Joseph saw the prophecies fulfilled in Jesus. He stepped forward braving all risks and took his stand for Jesus. A remarkable courage! A courage stirred by the death of Jesus.

Thought 1. Every secret believer needs to study the cross of Christ. Really seeing the cross will turn any secret believer into a bold witness for Christ.

Thought 2. Joseph courageously asked to take care of the physical body of Christ. Today, the body of Christ is the church. We are to boldly step forward and take care of the church. There are special times of need within the church when special courage is needed to step forward and show care. In those times a fresh look at the cross will be helpful and can be used by God to stir us.

"For I determined not to know any thing among you, save Jesus Christ, and him crucified" (2 Co.2:1).

"Knowing that he which raised up the Lord Jesus shall raise up us also by Jesus, and shall present us with you. For all things are for your sakes, that the abundant grace might through the thanksgiving of many redound to the glory of God" (2 Co.4:14-15).

"And that he died for all, that they which live should not henceforth live unto themselves, but unto him which died for them, and rose again" (2 Co.5:15).

6. He was a man who cared deeply for Jesus. The words and acts of these two verses express care and tenderness, love and affection, as well as courage and boldness. Joseph...
   • took the Lord's body down from the cross
   • wrapped the body in linen
   • laid the body in a tomb, a tomb wherein no man had ever been laid
   • acted quickly, before the Sabbath began. Jesus died at 3 p.m. Friday afternoon which was the day of preparation for the Sabbath (see Mk.15:33-34, 37). Work was forbidden on the Sabbath, so if anything was to be done with Jesus' body, it had to be done immediately. Only three hours remained for work. (See note—Mk.15:42 for more discussion.)

This act alone would leave no doubt about the effect of the cross upon Joseph. The cross changed his life. He was no longer a secret believer; he now demonstrated a public stand for Jesus.

Thought 1. Position, power, wealth, fame—none of these can make us bold for Christ. Only true affection for Christ will make us bold, and only as we see the cross of Christ will affection for Christ be aroused.

Thought 2. Christ identified with men perfectly.
   ⇒ He lived as a man—but perfectly.
   ⇒ He died as a man—but perfectly (as the Ideal Man).
   ⇒ He was buried as a man—but perfectly.

"And he made his grave with the wicked, and with the rich in his death; because he had done no violence, neither was any deceit in his mouth" (Is.53:9).

"Wherefore in all things it behoved him to be made like unto his brethren, that he might be a merciful and faithful high priest in things pertaining to God, to make reconciliation for the sins of the people" (He.2:17).

Thought 3. God's own Son possessed nothing when He was on earth; therefore when He died, He had to be buried in a borrowed tomb. Note two things.
   ⇒ Christ is the Savior of the poorest. He was born in a stable. He had no place of His own to lay His head (Mt.8:20; Lu.9:58). His tomb was a borrowed tomb.
   ⇒ Yet the rich can serve Him just as Joseph of Arimathaea did.

"And Jesus said unto him, Foxes have holes, and birds of the air have nests; but the Son of man hath not where to lay his head" (Lu.9:58).

27

"Sell that ye have, and give alms; provide yourselves bags which wax not old, a treasure in the heavens that faileth not, where no thief approacheth, neither moth corrupteth" (Lu.12:33).

"I have showed you all things, how that so labouring ye ought to support the weak, and to remember the words of the Lord Jesus, how he said, It is more blessed to give than to receive" (Ac.20:35).

"For ye know the grace of our Lord Jesus Christ, that, though he was rich, yet for your sakes he became poor, that ye through his poverty might be rich" (2 Co.8:9).

"Hereby preceive we the love of God, because he laid down his life for us: and we ought to lay down our lives for the brethren" (1 Jn.3:16).

[2] (23:55-56) **Jesus Christ, Love for—Eternal Life**: the women believers were stirred to loyalty and affection. Note three facts.

1. The women demonstrated a fearless loyalty despite all danger. At the cross the men forsook Jesus, but not the women (Mt.26:56, 69-75; see Mt.27:55-56, 61; Mk.15:41).

2. The women demonstrated a deep affection for Jesus. They took their own money to buy spices and ointments to embalm Jesus. This they did because they loved Him (Lu.23:56; see Mt.27:61; Mk.16:1).

3. The women did not yet understand the resurrection of Jesus. They were preparing His body to lie and eventually to decay in the tomb. The true meaning of *living forever—the human body being remade, recreated, and becoming incorruptible*—had not yet been grasped by them (Jn.5:24-29; see 1 Co.15:42f. See 1 Co.15:1-58.)

Thought 1. The testimony of these women should stir men to stand up for Christ. Too often it is the women who take the lead in standing forth for Christ. This should not be the case. Men...

- should be loyal to Christ, no matter how grave the danger.
- should love Christ to such an extent that they give all they *are and have* to Christ.
- should seek to understand and grasp the resurrection of Christ in all its fullness.

"Be not thou therefore ashamed of the testimony of our Lord" (2 Ti.1:8).

"For I am not ashamed of the gospel of Christ: for it is the power of God unto salvation to every one that believeth; to the Jew first, and also to the Greek" (Ro.1:16).

	CHAPTER 24	them, Why seek ye the living among the dead?	
	XII. THE SON OF MAN'S GLORY: HIS RESURRECTION & ASCENSION, 24:1-53	6 He is not here, but is risen: remember how he spake unto you when he was yet in Galilee,	c. Their proclamation d. Their reminder of Jesus' prophecy
	A. Jesus' Empty Tomb: Its Discovery, 24:1-12 *(Mt. 28:1-15; Mk. 16:1-11; Jn. 20:1-18)*	7 Saying, The Son of man must be delivered into the hands of sinful men, and be crucified, and the third day rise again. 8 And they remembered his words,	
1. The first day of the week **2. The first witness of the resurrection**	Now upon the first day of the week, very early in the morning, they came unto the sepulchre, bringing the spices which they had prepared, and certain others with them.	9 And returned from the sepulchre, and told all these things unto the eleven, and to all the rest. 10 It was Mary Magdalene, and Joanna, and Mary the mother of James, and other women that were with them, which told these things unto the apostles.	**6. The immediate unbelief of the apostles** a. The message of the resurrection was carried by women—initially
3. The great stone rolled away **4. The body missing from the tomb**	2 And they found the stone rolled away from the sepulchre. 3 And they entered in, and found not the body of the Lord Jesus.	11 And their words seemed to them as idle tales, and they believed them not.	b. The message of the resurrection was perceived as nonsense & denied
5. The two angels & their unbelievable message a. Their dazzling clothes b. Their question	4 And it came to pass, as they were much perplexed thereabout, behold, two men stood by them in shining garments: 5 And as they were afraid, and bowed down their faces to the earth, they said unto	12 Then arose Peter, and ran unto the sepulchre; and stooping down, he beheld the linen clothes laid by themselves, and departed, wondering in himself at that which was come to pass.	**7. The continued unbelief of Peter** a. He ran to see—hopeful b. He saw evidence: Linen clothes folded & off to the side c. He wondered

DIVISION XII

THE SON OF MAN'S GLORY: HIS RESURRECTION AND ASCENSION, 24:1-53

A. Jesus' Empty Tomb: Its Discovery, 24:1-12

(24:1-12) **Introduction**: the tomb was empty. Discovering the empty tomb was the greatest discovery in human history. However, the great tragedy is that most people either are not aware that Jesus arose or do not believe that He arose. Every man has to discover the fact for himself. The empty tomb and the risen Lord have to become a personal discovery for every man.

1. The first day of the week (v.1).
2. The first witnesses of the resurrection (v.1).
3. The great stone rolled away (v.2).
4. The body's missing from the tomb (v.3).
5. The two angels and their unbelievable message (vv.4-8).
6. The immediate unbelief of the apostles (vv.9-11).
7. The continued unbelief of Peter (v.12).

1 (24:1) **Jesus Christ, Resurrection**: the first day of the week, Sunday, was the day upon which Jesus arose, the day after the Jewish Sabbath (Saturday). Note three facts.

1. Luke clearly spells out when Jesus arose: "Upon the first day of the week, very early in the morning." Jesus arose before dawn, before the sun arose on Sunday morning. This was significant to the early Christian believers, so significant that they broke away from the common day for worship during the week, the Sabbath or Saturday. They began to worship on Sunday, the day of the resurrection of their Lord (see Ac.20:7; 1 Co.16:2).

2. Jesus arose on the first day of the week, on Sunday morning. This means that He had been in the grave for three days just as He had said (Mt.12:40; 16:21; 17:23; 20:19; Mk.9:31; 10:34; Lu.9:22; 18:33; 24:7, 46). His resurrection from the dead was a triumph, a conquest over death. Death reigns no more—its rule has been broken (1 Co.15:55-56; 2 Co.1:9-10; 2 Ti.1:10; He.2:9, 14-15).

3. Again, Jesus arose on the first day of the week, Sunday morning. He was in the grave on the Sabbath, unable to observe the laws governing the great season of the Passover and the Sabbath. He was dead; therefore, the law and its observances had no authority over Him. This is symbolic of the *identification* believers gain in Christ. When a man believes in Jesus Christ, God identifies the man with Christ, in particular with the death of Christ. God counts the man as having died

with Christ. Very simply, *in Christ's death* believers become dead to the law (see notes—Ro.7:4; Mt.5:17-18 for more discussion).

[2] (24:1) **Jesus Christ, Resurrection**: the first witnesses of the resurrection provide strong evidence of the resurrection.

1. They were actual witnesses of Jesus' *death and burial*. They knew He was dead, and they knew where He had been laid. They had followed along behind the procession to the tomb (Mt.15:40-41, 47; see Mt.27:55-56, 61; Lu.23:55-56). There was no question whatsoever in their mind about His being dead and buried.

2. They had purchased spices and had *come to anoint* Jesus' body. Apparently they had bought the spices Saturday evening after 6 p.m. when the Sabbath ended. Note: they arose "very early in the morning, the first day of the week [Sunday]" to go and embalm Him. Again, they knew He was dead, and they cared; so they wanted to take care of His body just as loved ones care for the bodies of their deceased.

3. They were religionists who *strictly obeyed the law*. They were strict in the observance of the Sabbath. Imagine—their loved one was dead, yet they would not break the Sabbath law even to take care of Him (see Lu.23:56). The women were obedient to the commandments of God. They were *moral and truthful* and would never think, much less consider, lying about the death and resurrection of Jesus.

[3] (24:2) **Jesus Christ, Resurrection**: the great stone was rolled away from the entrance (see DEEPER STUDY # 1, *Stone*—Mt.27:65-66). The rolled away stone perplexed the women (v.4). However, the stone had not been rolled back for the benefit of Jesus, but for the witnesses to the resurrection. When Jesus arose, He was in His resurrection body, the heavenly body of the spiritual dimension; and the spiritual dimension has no physical bounds. But the witnesses needed to enter the tomb and see the truth (see outline and notes—Jn.20:1-10).

[4] (24:3) **Jesus Christ, Resurrection**: the body was missing from the tomb. The account is simple, yet striking: "They entered in, and found not the body of the Lord Jesus." They "beheld," saw, contemplated that Jesus was not there (Mk.16:6). They saw the slab upon which He had been laid, and *He was not there*.

> "And being fully persuaded that, what he had promised, he was able also to perform" (Ro.4:21).
> "For all the promises of God in him are yea, and in him Amen, unto the glory of God by us" (2 Co.1:20).
> "If we believe not, yet he abideth faithful: he cannot deny himself" (2 Ti.2:13).
> "Whereby are given unto us exceeding great and precious promises: that by these ye might be partakers of the divine nature, having escaped the corruption that is in the world through lust" (2 Pe.1:4).

[5] (24:4-8) **Angels—Jesus Christ, Resurrection**: two angels appeared with a message for the women. Note four significant points about the angels.

1. The angels were radiant, dazzling figures. Their garments shone (Mt.28:3)...
   * "like lightning" (visible, quick, startling, striking, frightening, brilliant)
   * "white as snow" (pure, glistening)

Note the women feared and fell down, bowing in reverence.

2. The angels asked a pointed question: "Why seek ye the living among the dead?" There was a rebuke in the question. They were seeking to honor a dead Savior, a Savior who was as all other men are, frail and powerless to do anything about life and eternity. Their whole being—their thoughts, feelings, and behavior—were focused upon a dead Savior.

They were living just as the world lives—"strangers from the covenants of promise, having no hope, and without God in the world" (Ep.2:12).

3. The angels proclaimed the glorious news: "He is not here, but is risen." Note two points.
   a. "He is not here": the women could see and did see the fact. The fact was clearly evident: Jesus was not in the tomb. He had been there, for the women had seen Him put there. They had witnessed His death and burial, but He was no longer in the tomb (see note—Lu.23:55-56).
   b. "He is risen." Startling, unbelievable words...
      * yet, heaven "witnessed that He liveth" (He.7:8).
      * yet, Scripture witnesses that He arose (Ro.1:4; Ep.1:19-20).
      * yet, He had foretold that He would arise (Lu.9:22; 13:32; 17:25; 18:31-34).

> "And declared to be the Son of God with power, according to the spirit of holiness, by the resurrection from the dead" (Ro.1:4).
> "And what is the exceeding greatness of his power to usward who believe, according to the working of his mighty power, which he wrought in Christ, when he raised him from the dead, and set him at his own right hand in the heavenly places" (Ep.1:19-20).

4. The angels reminded the women that Jesus had foretold His death and resurrection (see outline and notes—Lu.18:31-34). Note the words, "And they remembered His words." The followers of Jesus had always been confused about the

prophecy of His death and resurrection. They *would not* accept his words literally, refusing to take His predictions at face value. They symbolized His statements; therefore, they never understood His death and resurrection (see note—Lu.18:34).

But note what happened now. They knew they had been wrong. Conviction struck them, and they became the very first witnesses to the resurrection.

> "But Jesus beheld them, and said unto them, With men this is impossible; but with God all things are possible" (Mt.19:26).
> "For with God nothing shall be impossible" (Lu.1:37).
> "God is faithful, by whom ye were called unto the fellowship of his Son Jesus Christ our Lord" (1 Co.1:9).
> "If we believe not, yet he abideth faithful: he cannot deny himself" (2 Ti.2:13).
> "Let us hold fast the profession of our faith without wavering; (for he is faithful that promised)" (He.10:23).

6 (24:9-11) **Unbelief—Disciples**: the disciples were quick to express their disbelief. The women rushed to the disciples to share the glorious news. But the news "seemed to them as idle tales" (hos leros): nonsense, ridiculous talk, wild imagination. "They believed them not." The Greek word is *disbelieved* (epistoun) and is in the imperfect active tense which means they "*kept on disbelieving,*" kept on putting no trust or confidence in what the women were claiming. They were *gripped* with a skeptical, unbelieving spirit.

Thought 1. The disciples were without excuse. Christ had spent month after month drilling His death and resurrection into His disciples. (See notes—Mt.16:21-28; 17:1-13; 17:22; 17:24-27 for more discussion.)

> "Afterward he appeared unto the eleven as they sat at meat, and upbraided them with their unbelief and hardness of heart, because they believed not them which had seen him after he was risen" (Mk.16:14).
> "He that believeth on him is not condemned: but he that believeth not is condemned already, because he hath not believed in the name of the only begotten Son of God" (Jn.3:18).
> "Take heed, brethren, lest there be in any of you an evil heart of unbelief, in departing from the living God" (He.3:12).
> "Let us labour therefore to enter into that rest, lest any man fall after the same example of unbelief" (He.4:11).

7 (24:12) **Unbelief—Peter**: Peter continued on in his unbelief. Peter's heart was still drawn to the Lord despite his enormous failure. Hearing that the body of Jesus was no longer in the tomb, he rushed to the tomb with his thoughts flying, wondering what had happened to the Lord.

Note a crucial point. Peter stooped down and saw the evidence: the linen clothes were lying off to the side by themselves. However, Peter did not grasp the significance of the evidence. John said he had rushed to the tomb with Peter and did believe, based upon the evidence of the linen clothes. He also verifies that Peter did not grasp the significance at this point (see note—Jn.20:1-10 for a discussion of this significant point). Peter just "departed," wondering within himself what had really happened.

Thought 1. It is dangerous not to understand the Lord's Word, not to take His Word at face value. Spiritualizing His words, unless the words are clearly symbolic, often leads to serious unbelief and problems.

Thought 2. A person has to be open to the evidence of the resurrection. The tomb is empty; He is risen—and the honest and seeking man will be convinced by the Spirit of God. What is needed is to do as Peter did: run to the tomb to see what really did happen.

> "Then he said unto them, O fools, and slow of heart to believe all that the prophets have spoken" (Lu.24:25).
> "And he said unto them, Why are ye so fearful? how is it that ye have no faith?" (Mk.4:40).
> "He that believeth on the Son hath everlasting life: and he that believeth not the Son shall not see life; but the wrath of God abideth on him" (Jn.3:36).
> "I said therefore unto you, that ye shall die in your sins: for if ye believe not that I am he, ye shall die in your sins" (Jn.8:24).

B. Jesus' Appearance to Two Believers on the Road to Emmaus: An Immortal Journey, 24:13-35

(Mk. 16:12-13)

1. **Scene 1: Two disciples taking a lonely & preoccupied walk**[DS1]
   a. They had heard about the resurrection: "That same day"
   b. They thought about & discussed the events

2. **Scene 2: Considering three critical questions**

   a. Jesus drew near, but they did not recognize Him

   b. Jesus 1st question: What are you talking about?
      1) Attitude: Gloomy

      2) Answer: The things that have happened

   c. Jesus 2nd question: What events?
      1) Jesus' death
         • He was a great prophet

         • He was crucified

         • He was thought to be the Messiah
      2) Jesus' prophecy of three days

      3) Jesus' empty tomb & perplexing reports

13 And, behold, two of them went that same day to a village called Emmaus, which was from Jerusalem about threescore furlongs.
14 And they talked together of all these things which had happened.
15 And it came to pass, that, while they communed together and reasoned, Jesus himself drew near, and went with them.
16 But their eyes were holden that they should not know him.
17 And he said unto them, What manner of communications are these that ye have one to another, as ye walk, and are sad?
18 And the one of them, whose name was Cleopas, answering said unto him, Art thou only a stranger in Jerusalem, and hast not known the things which are come to pass there in these days?
19 And he said unto them, What things? And they said unto him, Concerning Jesus of Nazareth, which was a prophet mighty in deed and word before God and all the people:
20 And how the chief priests and our rulers delivered him to be condemned to death, and have crucified him.
21 But we trusted that it had been he which should have redeemed Israel: and beside all this, to day is the third day since these things were done.
22 Yea, and certain women also of our company made us astonished, which were early at the sepulchre;

23 And when they found not his body, they came, saying, that they had also seen a vision of angels, which said that he was alive.
24 And certain of them which were with us went to the sepulchre, and found it even so as the women had said: but him they saw not.
25 Then he said unto them, O fools, and slow of heart to believe all that the prophets have spoken:
26 Ought not Christ to have suffered these things, and to enter into his glory?
27 And beginning at Moses and all the prophets, he expounded unto them in all the scriptures the things concerning himself.
28 And they drew nigh unto the village, whither they went: and he made as though he would have gone further.
29 But they constrained him, saying, Abide with us: for it is toward evening, and the day is far spent. And he went in to tarry with them.
30 And it came to pass, as he sat at meat with them, he took bread, and blessed it, and brake, and gave to them.
31 And their eyes were opened, and they knew him; and he vanished out of their sight.
32 And they said one to another, Did not our heart burn within us, while he talked with us by the way, and while he opened to us the scriptures?
33 And they rose up the same hour, and returned to Jerusalem, and found the eleven gathered together, and them that were with them,
34 Saying, The Lord is risen indeed, and hath appeared to Simon.
35 And they told what things were done in the way, and how he was known of them in breaking of bread.

• Reports of visions
• Reports of Jesus' being alive
• Reports confirmed

d. Question 3: Did not the prophets predict the Messiah's death & resurrection?
   1) Jesus mildly rebuked them
   2) Jesus' death & resurrection were necessary

   3) Jesus explained the Scripture

3. **Scene 3: Experiencing the burning truth—Jesus is risen; He is alive**

   a. The two sought to hear more: Invited Him to stay with them
      1) He accepted the invitation

      2) He blessed the food

   b. God opened their eyes: They knew the Lord, but He disappeared from their sight

   c. They had experienced conviction: A burning within their hearts

4. **Scene 4: Proclaiming the immortal witness**
   a. The two rushed to the disciples

   b. The exciting meeting, the immortal witness: Christ is risen
      1) Had been seen by Simon
      2) Had been seen by the two from Emmaus

DIVISION XII

THE SON OF MAN'S GLORY: HIS RESURRECTION AND ASCENSION, 24:1-53

B. Jesus' Appearance to Two Believers on the Road to Emmaus: An Immortal Journey, 24:13-35

(24:13-35) **Introduction**: this is one of the most beloved accounts of the resurrection story. It is an account of Jesus' helping two ordinary persons who had lost hope and fallen into the pit of sadness and despair. Their experience was an immortal journey.

LUKE 24:13-35

1. Scene 1: taking a lonely but thoughtful walk (vv.13-14).
2. Scene 2: considering three critical questions (vv.15-27).
3. Scene 3: experiencing the burning truth—Jesus is risen; He is alive (vv.28-32).
4. Scene 4: proclaiming the immortal witness (vv.33-35).

1 (24:13-14) **Hopelessness—Despair—Devastation**: the first scene was that of a lonely walk by two people who were sad, despairing, and very preoccupied.

The day is important: it was "that same day" that the women discovered the empty tomb and reported it to the disciples (the resurrection day, Easter Sunday). The news had been received with skepticism, as utter nonsense. These two, Cleopas and his companion, had either been present or else had heard the news from some other source. As they made their way to Emmaus they were sad, gripped by a spirit of despair over the Lord's crucifixion. Their hope that Jesus was the promised Messiah had been devastated, dashed against the rocks of death. But in their despair, their thoughts were rushing wildly about, entangled, wondering about the report of the women concerning the empty tomb and the angels. What did it mean?

The point to note is their emotions and thoughts, their...
- sadness and despair (over the Lord's death)
- devastated hope (in believing that Jesus was not the Messiah)
- rushing and entangled thoughts (over the reports of an empty tomb and angels)

Thought 1. The scene is a symbol of the despair that grips so many in life. Their hopes are devastated, hopes for...
- family
- school
- meaning and purpose
- profession
- acceptance

In their sadness and despair, somewhere, they hear reports of the empty tomb and of the living Lord; but they do not know what the reports mean, not personally.

"My soul is weary of my life; I will leave my complaint upon myself; I will speak in the bitterness of my soul" (Jb. 10:1).
"For my life is spent with grief, and my years with sighing: my strength faileth because of mine iniquity, and my bones are consumed" (Ps.31:10).
"O my God, my soul is cast down within me" (Ps.42:6).
"I sink in deep mire, where there is no standing: I am come into deep waters, where the floods overflow me" (Ps.69:2).
"But as for me, my feet were almost gone; my steps had well-nigh slipped" (Ps.73:2).
"When I thought to know this, it was too painful for me" (Ps.73:16).
"By the rivers of Babylon, there we sat down, yea, we wept, when we remembered Zion" (Ps.137:1).
"The LORD hath forsaken me, and my Lord hath forgotten me" (Is.49:14).
"Withhold thy foot from being unshod, and thy throat from thirst: but thou saidst, There is no hope: no; for I have loved strangers, and after them will I go" (Je.2:25).
"But I would not have you to be ignorant, brethren, concerning them which are asleep [dead], that ye sorrow not, even as others which have no hope" (1 Th.4:13).
"That at that time ye were without Christ...having no hope, and without God in the world" (Ep.2:12).

DEEPER STUDY # 1
(24:13) **Emmaus**: the city and location are unknown. It was about seven miles out of Jerusalem, which would take somewhere around two hours to travel by foot.

---

2 (24:15-27) **Jesus Christ, Death—Misconception—Puzzlement—Questioning—Perplexity**: the second scene was consideration of three questions. Note the exact words as Cleopas and his companion walked along: "*While* they communed together and reasoned, Jesus Himself drew near, and *went with them*" (suneporeueto, imperfect tense). The idea is that they were so absorbed in their despair and talk that Jesus *was already* walking along with them when they noticed Him. But note: they did not know Him. His resurrected body differed enough that He was not recognized as Jesus without close observation (see DEEPER STUDY # 1—Jn.21:1). In this particular instance, the Lord "held" (restrained, kept) their eyes from recognizing Him as well. Apparently He wanted them to more freely discuss the events with Him.

1. The first question: What are you talking about; what is it that is causing you to look so *sad* (skuthropoi)? The Greek word means gloomy, dejected, despondent, sullen, overcast. Jesus could see sadness and despair written all over their faces.

Cleopas was surprised that the stranger did not know. "How could anyone be in Jerusalem and not know why we are sad and despairing?" he asked. Terrible things had happened.

Thought 1. These two were seeking to understand the death and empty tomb of Christ. Christ was the subject of their conversation. They were seeking the truth; therefore, Christ drew near them.

"Ask, and it shall be given you; seek, and ye shall find; knock, and it shall be opened unto you: for every one that asketh receiveth; and he that seeketh findeth; and to him that knocketh it shall be opened" (Mt.7:7-8).

33

"Then said Jesus to those Jews which believed on him, If ye continue in my word, then are ye my disciples indeed; and ye shall know the truth, and the truth shall make you free" (Jn.8:31-32).

2. The second question: "What events? What circumstances could possibly cause such sadness and despair?" (v.19-24). Cleopas answered, covering three subjects.

a. Jesus' death.
⇒ He was a great prophet.
⇒ The rulers crucified him. (Note the whole world is implicated. The Jews delivered Him, and the Gentile Romans condemned and crucified Him.)
⇒ We had *trusted* (elpizomen, hoped) that He was the Messiah, the One who was to save Israel.

b. Jesus' prophecy of three days. There is significance in the term "three days." Cleopas was sharing how their *dead Master* had told them...
• to watch for the third day, for some unusual event.
• that He had spoken of "rising again on the third day," whatever that meant.
• that they thought the words meant that His triumph would take place on the third day. (See outline and notes—Lu.18:31-34 for more discussion.)

c. Jesus' empty tomb and perplexing reports from certain women, reports...
• of an empty tomb
• of a vision of angels
• of Jesus' being alive
• that had been confirmed
• that Jesus was not seen

Thought 1. World events and the terrible things that happen in life often make a person sad and despairing—such things as...

• being misunderstood	• helplessness	• loss
• being opposed	• death	• fear
• being deserted	• hopelessness	• injustice
• being betrayed	• divisiveness	

Christ is concerned. He wants to know what it is that causes so much sadness and despair. He wants us to share our problems with Him.

Thought 2. The problem with the two from Emmaus, as it is with so many today, was their *shortsightedness* and *unbelief*.

Thought 3. There is one major reason why men refuse to accept a risen Lord. A risen Lord means that a man must subject himself to the Lord and obey and serve Him.

> **"Therefore let all the house of Israel know assuredly, that God hath made that same Jesus, whom ye have crucified, both Lord and Christ" (Ac.2:36).**
> **"Him hath God exalted with his right hand to be a Prince and a Saviour, for to give repentance to Israel, and forgiveness of sins. And we are his witnesses of these things; and so is also the Holy Ghost, whom God hath given to them that obey him" (Ac.5:31-32).**
> **"Wherefore God also hath highly exalted him, and given him a name which is above every name" (Ph.2:9).**

Thought 4. Every man should be engrossed in the death of Christ, but he should also believe and be engrossed in the resurrection of the Lord.

> **"Who was delivered for our offences, and was raised again for our justification" (Ro.4:25).**
> **"Who is he that condemneth? It is Christ that died, yea rather, that is risen again, who is even at the right hand of God, who also maketh intercession for us" (Ro.8:34).**
> **"Wherefore he is able also to save them to the uttermost that come unto God my him, seeing he ever liveth to make intercession for them" (He.7:25).**

3. The third question: "Did not the prophets predict Messiah's death and resurrection?" (v.25-27). Note several facts.

a. Jesus rebuked the two disciples for being dull and slow to believe. He called them *fools* (anoetoi), which means that they were dull and slow to believe. More was expected of them; they should have known more than they were indicating. They were without excuse, for their minds and hearts were capable of more. Therefore, Jesus rebuked them for being...
• *slow to believe*
• slow to believe *all* the prophets had spoken

b. Jesus shared that the death and resurrection of the Messiah was a necessity. The words *ought not* (ouchi edei) are strong. They mean there was a constraint, an imperative, a necessity laid upon the Messiah to die and arise. He had no choice. His death and resurrection had been planned and willed by God through all eternity. Therefore, He had to fulfill the will of God, for God had ordained...

- that the Messiah suffer these things.
- that the Messiah enter into His glory. God's plan was not defeated. He conquered through the death of His Son, the Messiah.

c. Jesus explained the Scripture to the two disciples, taught them book by book, showing them the things concerning the Messiah in each book. Note the words "all the scriptures." Prophecies of Christ are found in all the Scripture; therefore, Jesus carried the two disciples through the Scripture in a systematic way, book by book, showing them how God's purpose was fulfilled in the death of the Messiah. The two disciples could now be saved eternally, not just during an earthly reign of an earthly Messiah.

Thought 1. The two disciples were feeling hopeless and perplexed, full of sadness and despair for one very simple reason: unbelief. They had *symbolized* or *spiritualized* the Scripture and the clear predictions which Jesus had given his disciples before His death. Therefore, they could not see *beyond* Jesus' death. They were willing to accept and admire a *dead Savior*, a great prophet who had been martyred, but they had great difficulty in accepting a risen Lord. They would not believe the reports of the women, the glorious news of the living Lord.

> **"And their words seemed to them as idle tales, and they believed them not" (Lu.24:11).**
> **"Let us labour therefore to enter into that rest, lest any man fall after the same example of unbelief" (He.4:11).**
> **"For consider him that endured such contradiction of sinners against himself, lest ye be wearied and faint in your minds" (He.12:3).**

[3] (24:28-32) **Conviction—Conversion**: the third scene was experiencing the burning truth—Jesus is risen and alive forevermore. Note three important points.

1. The two disciples *sought* to hear more. They invited Jesus to abide with them. The words "made as though" do not mean Jesus was play-acting. He never pretends. He would have gone on, for He never enters a life or a home without a personal invitation. The two were seeking the truth, so they wanted Jesus to enter their home and to share more with them. (How unlike so many today!)

Jesus did enter, and He sat down to have dinner with them. He was also asked to give thanks for the meal.

2. God opened the eyes of the two disciples. They immediately knew the Lord. But note why: they had invited Jesus into their home. If they had let Him pass on, the likelihood is that they would never have known it was the Lord.

3. The two disciples had experienced a burning conviction within their hearts.

a. The Word of God being proclaimed is what had stirred the conviction and the burning.

> **"Wherefore thus saith the LORD God of hosts, Because ye speak this word, behold, I will make my words in thy mouth fire, and this people wood, and it shall devour them" (Je.5:14).**
> **"Is not my word like as a fire? saith the LORD; and like a hammer that breaketh the rock in pieces?" (Je.23:29).**

b. Their response to the conviction—inviting Christ into their home—led to their coming to know Him personally.

> **"Behold, I stand at the door, and knock: if any man hear my voice, and open the door, I will come in to him, and will sup with him, and he with me" (Re.3:20).**
> **"God is faithful, by whom ye were called unto the fellowship of his Son Jesus Christ our Lord" (1 Co.1:9).**
> **"For where two or three are gathered together in my name, there am I in the midst of them" (Mt.18:20).**

Thought 1. The two had heard the Scripture explained, and they had heard much. But they had to respond, to invite the Lord into their home before God could open their eyes and bring them to a knowledge of Christ.

[4] (24:33-35) **Jesus Christ, Resurrection**: the fourth scene was proclaiming the immortal witness. The scene was dramatic. It was night, but the two rushed back to the apostles. When they arrived, they found the apostles and some other disciples already gathered together.

They were all bursting with excitement. To the shock of the two from Emmaus, the group had the same immortal witness to share: "The Lord is risen. He has appeared to Simon." As they listened to Simon's experience, they were bursting at the seams, hardly able to contain themselves, waiting to share their own experience.

Finally, their time came to share their experience and the very same immortal witness: "The Lord is risen indeed."

> **"And ye also shall bear witness, because ye have been with me from the beginning" (Jn.15:27).**
> **"Thou shall be his witness unto all men of what thou hast seen and heard" (Ac.22:15).**
> **"And we are witnesses of all things which he did both in the land of the Jews, and in Jerusalem; whom they slew and hanged on a tree: Him God raised up the third day, and showed him openly" (Ac.10:39-40).**

1. The first statement: Jesus is risen	C. Jesus' Appearance to the Disciples: The Great Statements of the Christian Faith, 24:36-49	an honeycomb.	2. The second statement: All
	(Mk. 16:14; Jn. 20:19-23; 20:26-21:25)	43 And he took it, and did eat before them.	Scripture must be fulfilled
		44 And he said unto them, These are the words which I spake unto you, while I was yet with you, that all things must be fulfilled, which were written in the law of Moses, and in the prophets, and in the psalms, concerning me.	a. The forewarning
			b. The utter necessity
a. Jesus' first words: Peace	36 And as they thus spake, Jesus himself stood in the midst of them, and saith unto them, Peace be unto you.		
b. Jesus' impact	37 But they were terrified and affrighted, and supposed that they had seen a spirit.	45 Then opened he their understanding, that they might understand the scriptures,	c. The spiritual insight needed to understand the Scriptures
1) The disciples were startled & frightened			
2) The disciples were troubled & silently questioning what they were seeing	38 And he said unto them, Why are ye troubled? and why do thoughts arise in your hearts?	46 And said unto them, Thus it is written, and thus it behoved Christ to suffer, and to rise from the dead the third day:	d. The particular prophecies that must be understood
c. Jesus' proof[DS1]	39 Behold my hands and my feet, that it is I myself: handle me, and see; for a spirit hath not flesh and bones, as ye see me have.		1) Christ must suffer & arise
1) He is flesh & bones		47 And that repentance and remission of sins should be preached in his name among all nations, beginning at Jerusalem.	2) Repentance & forgiveness must be preached
2) He showed them his wounds	40 And when he had thus spoken, he showed them his hands and his feet.	48 And ye are witnesses of these things.	
3) He talked	41 And while they yet believed not for joy, and wondered, he said unto them, Have ye here any meat?	49 And, behold, I send the promise of my Father upon you: but tarry ye in the city of Jerusalem, until ye be endued with power from on high.	3) The Holy Spirit & His power must be sent
4) He ate	42 And they gave him a piece of a broiled fish, and of		

DIVISION XII

THE SON OF MAN'S GLORY: HIS RESURRECTION AND ASCENSION, 24:1-53

C. Jesus' Appearance to the Disciples: The Great Statements of the Christian Faith, 24:36-49

(24:36-49) **Introduction**: this was the first appearance of Jesus to *all the disciples at once*. He shared the two great statements (explanations) of the Christian faith.
 1. The first statement: Jesus is risen (vv.36-43).
 2. The second statement: all Scripture must be fulfilled (vv.44-49).

(24:36-49) **Another Outline**: The Great Statements of the Christian Faith.
 1. Statement 1: Jesus is risen (vv.36-43).
 2. Statement 2: All prophetic Scripture must be fulfilled (vv.44-46).
  a. The whole Old Testament.
  b. The death and resurrection of Christ.
 3. Statement 3: Repentance and forgiveness of sin are imperative (vv.47-48).
  a. The place: Among all nations.
  b. The witnesses: You—disciples.
 4. Statement 4: Power is to come upon you (v.49).
  a. The power is the Holy Spirit
  b. The power is given by tarrying (praying).

[1] (24:36-43) **Jesus Christ, Resurrection; Impact of; World Response to**: statement one is that Jesus is risen. The scene took place at night—the night of the very day of the Lord's resurrection. It was a dramatic scene. The Lord had already made at least four appearances. The four appearances named were to...
 • Mary Magdalene (Jn.20:14f)
 • the women visiting the tomb (Mt.28:1f; Mk.16:1f)
 • the two walking to Emmaus (Lu.24:1f)
 • Simon Peter (Lu.24:34; 1 Co.15:5)

The apostles (minus Thomas) and some other disciples had rushed to the known meeting place. The very air was electric. Excitement beat in the chest of every one, and minds were grasping for understanding. Wonder was beginning to overcome sadness and despair, and hope was beginning to stir great anticipation. Reports of appearances were being buzzed about and argued about. Then all of a sudden out of nowhere, into the very midst of all this, *"Christ Himself stood."* Note three things:

1. The very first words Jesus spoke to the disciples after His death: "Peace be unto you." This was the regular greeting of the Jews of that day, but it had a very special significance now. The disciples needed peace, the peace that only He could give. And He had now risen from the dead to give that peace to them. (See note, *Peace*—Jn.14:27.)

> **"But now in Christ Jesus ye who sometimes were far off are made nigh by the blood of Christ. For he is our peace, who hath made both one, and hath broken down the middle wall of partition between us" (Ep.2:13-14).**
> **"Peace I leave with you, my peace I give unto you: not as the world giveth, give I unto you. Let not your heart be troubled, neither let it be afraid" (Jn.14:27).**
> **"These things I have spoken unto you, that in me ye might have peace. In the world ye shall have tribulation: but be of good cheer; I have overcome the world" (Jn.16:33).**

2. The impact of Christ's resurrection. The disciples interpreted His sudden appearance in their midst just as they had always interpreted His words—spiritually. When He suddenly appeared, the immediate thought flashing across their minds was that a spirit was appearing to them. They were...
- terrified, frightened, and troubled
- questioning

Thought 1. Unbelievers respond to the resurrection in five ways.
1) They are terrified, frightened, and troubled by the resurrection. Why? Because it means they must obey and serve Christ. If He is the *living Lord*, then man is His subject.
2) They question the resurrection, the truth of it. The idea that a man could arise from the dead is beyond their acceptance.
3) They ignore the resurrection, pay no attention to it, and count it as being meaningless.
4) They respond to the resurrection, accepting Jesus Christ as their Savior and Lord.
5) They react to the resurrection—react all the way from mild opposition and cursing to the persecution of any who bear witness to the resurrection.

3. The proof of Christ's resurrection, that He had risen bodily. The outline of the Scripture above shows the four things Christ did to prove that it really was He and not a spirit who stood before the disciples (see DEEPER STUDY # 1—Lu.24:39-43 for discussion).

DEEPER STUDY # 1

(24:39-43) **Jesus Christ, Resurrection—Resurrection, Body of**: the risen Christ was not a spirit (v.39); not a vision, a phantom, an hallucination, or any other figment of man's imagination. He was the risen Lord—bodily—not someone else nor some other spirit. His body was none other than that of Jesus, the carpenter from Nazareth. He had physically risen from the dead and His body was real. It differed, yes, but it was His body. It was perfected and no longer subject to the limitations and frailties of the physical universe and its laws; it was now glorified by the power and spoken Word of God (see Ro.1:3-4).

How did the Lord's resurrected body differ from His earthly body? Some idea can be gleaned by looking at His resurrected body and the glorified body promised to the believer.

1. The resurrected body of the Lord was His body, but it was radically changed. It had all the appearance of a physical body, but it was not bound by the physical world and its material substance.
   a. It was the same body, not some other body. We know this because His resurrected body bore the marks of the nails in His hands and feet (Jn.20:20, 27), and the disciples could recognize Him after close observation.
   b. It was a body that could travel and appear anyplace, at will and by thought—a body unhampered by space, time, material, or substance. When He appeared it was suddenly, even behind locked doors (Lu.24:36; Jn.20:19).
   c. It was a body that differed enough that it was not clearly recognized at first, not until it was closely observed.
     ⇒ Mary Magdalene thought He was the gardener (Jn.20:15).
     ⇒ The two disciples walking toward Emmaus thought He was a traveler (Lu.24:31).
     ⇒ The disciples who were fishing did not recognize Him standing on the seashore (Jn.21:4).

   However, after close observation, the Lord was recognized in all these instances.
2. The resurrected, glorified body that is promised to the believer gives some additional insight into the kind of body Christ has. One of the most wonderful promises ever made to man is given in the words:

> **"Who shall change our vile body, that it may be fashioned like unto his glorious body, according to the working whereby he is able even to subdue all things unto himself" (Ph.3:21; see Mt.13:43; Ro.8:17; Col.3:4; Re.22:5).**
> **"[We shall be] conformed to the image of His Son" (Ro.8:29; see 1 Co.15:49; 2 Co.3:18).**
> **"Beloved, now are we the sons of God, and it doth not yet appear what we shall be: but we know that, when he shall appear, we shall be like him; for we shall see him as he is" (1 Jn.3:2).**

The body of the believer will undergo a radical change just as the Lord's body was radically changed. Several changes are promised the believer.

a. The believer shall receive a spiritual body.

> **"There is a natural body [soma psuchikon] and there is a spiritual body [som a pneumatikon]"** (1 Co.15:44).

Note: the spiritual body (soma) still retains the qualities of the earthly body (soma). The same Greek word is used for both bodies. The difference lies in that it will not be a natural (soulish) body but will be a spiritual body. What does this mean? In essence, the body will be perfected; no longer subject to pain, tears, death, sorrow, or crying (Re.14:4).
⇒ "It is sown in corruption; it is raised in incorruption."
⇒ "It is sown in dishonor; it is raised in glory."
⇒ "It is sown in weakness; it is raised in power."
⇒ "It is sown a natural body; it is raised a spiritual body."

Note that the body is the same body on earth that it will be in heaven. The body just undergoes a radical change of nature. The believer will be the same person in heaven that he is on earth, differing only in that he is perfected. Also note the strong, emphatic declaration: *There is* a natural body, and *there is* a spiritual body" (1 Co.15:42-44).

b. The believer shall receive a body that is not "flesh and blood." Flesh and blood are corruptible; they age, deteriorate, die and decay.

> **"Flesh and blood cannot inherit the kingdom of God; neither doth corruption inherit incorruption"** (1 Co.15:50).

c. The believer shall receive a body that shall be radically changed.

> **"In a moment, in the twinkling of an eye, at the last trump: for the trumpet shall sound, and the dead shall be raised incorruptible, and we shall be changed. For this corruptible must put on incorruption, and this mortal must put on immortality"** (1 Co.15:52-53).

d. The believer shall be given a body that will not need reproduction for continuing the (redeemed) human race.

> **"In the resurrection they neither marry, nor are given in marriage, but are as the angels of God in heaven"** (Mt.22:30).

---

2 (24:44-49) **Prophecy, Fulfilled—Jesus Christ, Death**: statement two is that all Scripture must be fulfilled. Note four points:
1. The forewarning Jesus had given in His predictions. His death and resurrection—the literal events happening just as He had said they would—should not have been a surprise. He had foretold the events and forewarned His followers. (See outline and notes—Lu.18:31-34.)

Thought 1. Scripture predicts much that is to happen in the future. However...
- some still will not accept and believe
- some still spiritualize the predictions

The greatest of all tragedies is that some still do not accept and believe the Lord's death and resurrection despite the irrefutable evidence.

2. The utter necessity that Christ die and arise. The word "must" (dei) means that His death was an imperative, a necessity, a constraint.

> **"Till heaven and earth pass, one jot or one tittle shall in no wise pass from the law, till all be fulfilled"** (Mt.5:18).
> **"Him, being delivered by the determinate counsel and foreknowledge of God, ye have taken, and by wicked hands have crucified and slain: whom God hath raised up, having loosed the pains of death: because it was not possible that he should be holden of it"** (Ac.2:23-24).
> **"And Paul, as his manner was, went in unto them, and three sabbath days reasoned with them out of the scriptures, opening and alleging, that Christ must needs have suffered, and risen again from the dead; and that this Jesus, whom I preach unto you, is Christ"** (Ac.17:2-3).

Note that Christ gave the three divisions of the Old Testament: the law, the prophets, and the psalms. The whole Old Testament prophesied of His coming and His salvation.
3. The spiritual insight needed to understand the Scriptures. Christ opened the disciples' eyes so they could understand.

> **"But the natural man receiveth not the things of the Spirit of God: for they are foolishness unto him: neither can he know them, because they are spiritually discerned"** (1 Co.2:14; see 1 Co.2:9-14).

4. The particular prophesies were threefold.
   a. Christ must suffer and arise (see outline and note—Lu.18:31-34).
   b. Repentance and forgiveness must be preached (see notes and DEEPER STUDY # 1—Ac.17:29-30; DEEPER STUDY # 4—Mt.26:28).
   c. The Holy Spirit and power must be sent. As the disciples went forth witnessing, they were to be given the *wonderful* promise (the Holy Spirit) and power of the Father. (See outline and notes, *Holy Spirit*—Jn.14:15-26; 16:7-15 for a discussion of the prophecies concerning the Holy Spirit which Christ had given to the disciples.) Note two points.
      1) The believer was to be equipped for witnessing.
         ⇒ He was to receive the promise of the Father (the Holy Spirit).
         ⇒ He was to receive power, being clothed (endusesthe) with power.
      2) The source of the spirit and power was God.
         ⇒ Christ was to send the promise.
         ⇒ The promise was "of the Father." God gave the promise.
         ⇒ Believers had to tarry, that is, wait upon the Lord and pray for the promise.
         ⇒ The promise was to come from "on high." God Himself was the Source of power for all evangelism.

   "But ye shall receive power, after that the Holy Ghost is come upon you: and ye shall be witnesses unto me both in Jerusalem, and in all Judaea, and in Samaria, and unto the uttermost part of the earth" (Ac.1:8).
   "And when he is come, he will reprove the world of sin, and of righteousness, and of judgment" (Jn.16:8).
   "Now unto him that is able to do exceeding abundantly above all that we ask or think, according to the power that worketh in us" (Ep.3:20).

	D. Jesus' Last Appearance: The Ascension,[DS1] 24:50-53 (Mk. 16:19-20; Ac.1:9-11)
1. The purpose of the ascension a. To bless His followers	50 And he led them out as far as to Bethany, and he lifted up his hands, and blessed them.
b. To provide a witness & give great assurance to His followers	51 And it came to pass, while he blessed them, he was parted from them, and carried up into heaven.

2. The disciples' response to the ascension
  a. Worshiped Him
  b. Were filled with joy
  c. Worshipped in the temple—continually
	52 And they worshipped him, and returned to Jerusalem with great joy:
	53 And were continually in the temple, praising and blessing God. Amen.

DIVISION XII

THE SON OF MAN'S GLORY: HIS RESURRECTION AND ASCENSION, 24:1-53

D. Jesus' Last Appearance: The Ascension, 24:50-53

(24:50-53) **Introduction**: Luke closes his gospel with the ascension of Christ and begins Acts with the ascension of Christ (Ac.1:9-11). The ascension closes the Lord's earthly ministry, His mission to save the world. Therefore, the ascension can be said to be the final chapter, the close, the consummation of His journey upon earth. On the other hand, the ascension opens the Lord's heavenly ministry, His mission of intercession for the world and His mission of bearing witness through the lives of believers. Therefore, the ascension can be said to be the first chapter, the opening, the beginning of His journey into heaven as the Risen Lord. In heaven, Jesus Christ is the risen Lord who is the propitiation "for the sins of the whole world" (1 Jn.2:1-2).

   1. The purpose of the ascension (vv.50-51).
   2. The disciples' response to the ascension (vv.52-53).

DEEPER STUDY # 1

(24:50-53) **Jesus Christ, Ascension**: the Lord ascended to the right hand of God, that is, to the position of sovereignty and power (see Mk.16:19; Lu.22:69; Ac.1:9-11; 2:36; 5:31; Ep.1:20; Ph.2:9-11; Re.5:12). The ascension assures (proves, confirms) that seven things are absolutely certain.

   1. The ascension assures that God *is*, that He is alive and does exist. The fact that Christ was raised up from the dead and "carried up into heaven" (Lu.24:51) proves that God is. Only God could do such a thing (1 Co.6:14; 2 Co.4:14; see Jn.3:16. See Ac.2:24, 32; 3:15, 26; 4:14; 5:30; 10:40; 13:30, 33-34; 17:31.)

   2. The ascension assures that Christ is God's Son. The very fact that God raised up Christ and "received [Him] up into heaven" proves that Christ is God's Son (Ro.1:3-4; Ph.2:5-11).

   3. The ascension assures that heaven is real (Ph.3:20-31).

   4. The ascension assures that the gospel is true. When God raised up Christ and received Him into heaven, God validated the message of Christ. What Christ proclaimed and revealed was true: man faces a critical problem, the problem of sin and death and a future of condemnation and separation from God. However, man can be saved by the cross of Christ (Mk.16:16; 1 Pe.2:24).

   5. The ascension assures that the Great Commission is the call and mission of believers. Two things show this. First, Christ has ascended into heaven; therefore, He is gone, no longer on earth. If the gospel is to be carried to the ends of the earth, believers have to do it. They are the ones left on earth to do it. Second, it is the risen and ascended Lord who gave the Great Commission. *As the ascended Lord*, He demands that His commission be fulfilled (Mk.16:15; see Mt.28:19-20).

   6. The ascension assures that power is available to carry out the Great Commission (Mt.28:18; see Mk.16:20).

   7. The ascension assures that we have a very special Helper in heaven, One who really loves and cares for us. He is One who is "touched with the feeling of our infirmities, [the One who was] in all points tempted like as we are, yet without sin" (He.4:15). Therefore, He is ever ready to forgive and to look after us through all of life.

---

1 (24:50-51) **Jesus Christ, Ascension**: the purpose of the ascension. Two general purposes are given by Luke (see note, *Ascension*—Ac.1:9).

   1. The first general purpose of the ascension was to bless the disciples. This was His final blessing, and note: it was the last thing He did on earth. His last gesture and act was to bless His disciples. This showed several things.
     a. It showed that He was the High Priest who had the power to make the sin-offering for them and to bless them with the gift of peace with God. (See *Aaron*, Le.9:22.)

"And Aaron lifted up his hand toward the people, and blessed them, and came down from offering of the sin offering, and the burnt offering, and peace offerings" (Le.9:22).

b. It showed that His blessing was the blessing coming from the ascended Lord who was *in heaven* exalted to the right hand of God.

"And what is the exceeding greatness of his power to us-ward who believe, according to the working of his mighty power, which he wrought in Christ, when he raised him from the dead, and set him at his own right hand in the heavenly places, far above all principality, and power, and might, and dominion, and every name that is named, not only in this world, but also in that which is to come" (Ep.1:19-21).
"Now unto him that is able to do exceeding abundantly above all that we ask or think, according to the power that worketh in us" (Ep.3:20).

c. It showed that His blessing was forever, without end, even to the end of the world.

"Teaching them to observe all things whatsoever I have commanded you: and, lo, I am with you away, even unto the end of the world" (Mt.28:20).

d. It showed that His blessing was unlimited, from their ascended and *eternal Lord*.

"And he is before all things, and by him all things consist" (Col.1:17).
"I am Alpha and Omega, the beginning and the end, the first and the last" (Re.22:13).

e. It showed that His blessing was upon them as they went forth as His representatives, witnessing for Him.

"Go ye therefore, and teach all nations, baptizing them in the name of the Father, and of the Son, and of the Holy Ghost: teaching them to observe all things whatsoever I have commanded you: and, lo, I am with you away, even unto the end of the world" (Mt.28:19-20).

2. The second general purpose of the ascension was to provide a witness and give great assurance (see DEEPER STUDY #1—Lu.24:50-53).

[2] (24:52-53) **Ascension, Results**: the disciples' response to the ascension was threefold.

1. The disciples worshipped Christ. The ascension stirred worship. Why? The disciples now knew beyond question that He was the true Messiah, the Son of God Himself. He had ascended to the right hand of God; therefore, He was due all the homage, adoration, and praise due God.

"Philip saith unto him, Lord, show us the Father, and it sufficeth us. Jesus saith unto him, Have I been so long time with you, and yet hast thou not known me, Philip? he that hath seen me hath seen the Father; and how sayest thou then, Show us the Father? Believest thou not that I am in the Father, and the Father in me?" (Jn.14:8-11).
"And being found in fashion as a man, he humbled himself, and became obedient unto death, even the death of the cross. Wherefore God also hath highly exalted him, and given him a name which is above every name: that at the name of Jesus every knee should bow, of things in heaven, and things in earth, and things under the earth; and that every tongue should confess that Jesus Christ is Lord, to the glory of God the Father" (Ph.2:8-11).

2. The disciples were filled with joy.
   a. They were filled with joy because their Lord was now exalted and privileged to take His rightful place: sitting at the right hand of God and being worshipped eternally. They were filled with joy and rejoicing *for Him*.
   b. They were filled with joy because they now knew that His presence would always be with them. When on earth physically, He could only be in one place and with only a few people at a time. But now, since ascending, He could send His Spirit to dwell with believers everywhere (Omnipresent). Nothing would ever again be able to *separate* their Lord from them.

"Nevertheless I tell you the truth; It is expedient for you that I go away: for if I go not away, the Comforter will not come unto you; but if I depart, I will send him unto you" (Jn.16:7).
"Who shall separate us from the love of Christ? shall tribulation, or distress, or persecution, or famine, or nakedness, or peril, or sword?...For I am persuaded, that neither death, nor life, nor angels, nor principalities, nor powers, nor things present, nor things to come, nor height, nor depth, nor any other creature, shall be able to separate us from the love of God, which is in Christ Jesus our Lord" (Ro.8:35, 38-39).

3. The disciples were in the temple continually. The temple was the focus of God's presence and worship, and it was the center of teaching, the place where the people were instructed in the Scriptures. The disciples were bound to focus their lives in the temple or church...

- because Christ had taught that the temple was His "Father's house" and "the house of prayer."

> "Saying unto them, It is written, My house is the house of prayer: but ye have made it a den of thieves" (Lu.19:46).
> "And said unto them that sold doves, Take these things hence; make not my Father's house an house of merchandise" (Jn.2:16).

- because they wished to praise God for sending the Messiah and to bear public testimony of Him.
- because the temple was the chosen place of God to manifest His presence among His people (see note—1 Co.3:16).

> "Go, stand and speak in the temple to the people all the words of this life" (Ac.5:20).
> "Not forsaking the assembling of ourselves together, as the manner of some is; but exhorting one another: and so much the more, as ye see the day approaching" (He.10:25).

OUTLINE BIBLE RESOURCES

This material, like similar works, has come from imperfect man and is thus susceptible to human error. We are nevertheless grateful to God for both calling us and empowering us through His Holy Spirit to undertake this task. Because of His goodness and grace, *The Preacher's Outline & Sermon Bible*® New Testament is complete and the Old Testament volumes are releasing periodically.

The Minister's Personal Handbook and other helpful **Outline Bible Resources** are available in printed form as well as releasing electronically on WORDsearch software.

God has given the strength and stamina to bring us this far. Our confidence is that as we keep our eyes on Him and grounded in the undeniable truths of the Word, we will continue working through the Old Testament volumes. The future includes other helpful Outline Bible Resources for God's dear servants to use in their Bible Study and discipleship.

We offer this material first to Him in whose Name we labor and serve and for whose glory it has been produced and, second, to everyone everywhere who preaches and teaches the Word.

Our daily prayer is that each volume will lead thousands, millions, yes even billions, into a better understanding of the Holy Scriptures and a fuller knowledge of Jesus Christ the Incarnate Word, of whom the Scriptures so faithfully testify.

You will be pleased to know that Leadership Ministries Worldwide partners with Christian organizations, printers, and mission groups around the world to make Outline Bible Resources available and affordable in many countries and foreign languages. It is our goal that *every* leader around the world, both clergy and lay, will be able to understand God's Holy Word and present God's message with more clarity, authority, and understanding—all beyond his or her own power.

LEADERSHIP MINISTRIES WORLDWIDE
PO Box 21310 • Chattanooga, TN 37424-0310
(423) 855-2181 • FAX (423) 855-8616
info@lmw.org
www.lmw.org - FREE Download materials

LEADERSHIP MINISTRIES WORLDWIDE

Publishers of Outline Bible Resources

• THE PREACHER'S OUTLINE & SERMON BIBLE® (POSB) • KJV – NIV

NEW TESTAMENT

Matthew 1 (chapters 1–15)
Matthew 2 (chapters 16–28)
Mark
Luke
John
Acts
Romans

1 & 2 Corinthians
Galatians, Ephesians, Philippians, Colossians
1 & 2 Thessalonians, 1 & 2 Timothy, Titus, Philemon
Hebrews, James
1 & 2 Peter, 1, 2, & 3 John, Jude
Revelation
Master Outline & Subject Index

OLD TESTAMENT

Genesis 1 (chapters 1–11)
Genesis 2 (chapters 12–50)
Exodus 1 (chapters 1–18)
Exodus 2 (chapters 19–40)
Leviticus
Numbers
Deuteronomy
Joshua
Judges, Ruth
1 Samuel
2 Samuel

1 Kings
2 Kings
1 Chronicles
2 Chronicles
Ezra, Nehemiah, Esther, Job
Psalms 1 (chapters 1-41)
Psalms 2 (chapters 42-106)
Psalms 3 (chapters 107-150)
Proverbs
Ecclesiastes, Song of Solomon

Isaiah 1 (chapters 1-35)
Isaiah 2 (chapters 36-66)
Jeremiah 1 (chapters 1-29)
Jeremiah 2 (chapters 30-52),
   Lamentations
Ezekiel
Daniel, Hosea
Joel, Amos, Obadiah, Jonah,
   Micah, Nahum
Habakkuk, Zephaniah, Haggai,
   Zechariah, Malachi

Print versions of all Outline Bible Resources are available in various forms.

- *What the Bible Says to the Believer* — **The Believer's Personal Handbook**
  11 Chs. – Over 500 Subjects, 300 Promises, & 400 Verses Expounded - Italian Imitation Leather or Paperback

- *What the Bible Says to the Minister* — **The Minister's Personal Handbook**
  12 Chs. - 127 Subjects - 400 Verses Expounded - Italian Imitation Leather or Paperback

- **Practical Word Studies In the New Testament** — 2 Vol. Hardcover Set

- **The Teacher's Outline & Study Bible™ - Various New Testament Books**
  Complete 30 - 45 minute lessons – with illustrations and discussion questions

- **Practical Illustrations — Companion to the POSB**
  Arranged by topic and Scripture reference

- **What the Bible Says About Series - Various Subjects**

- **OBR on various digital platforms**
  See current digital providers on our website at www.lmw.org

- **Translations of various books**
  See our website for more information or contact our office

— Contact LMW for quantity orders and information —

LEADERSHIP MINISTRIES WORLDWIDE or Your Local Christian Bookstore
PO Box 21310 • Chattanooga, TN 37424-0310
(423) 855-2181 • FAX (423) 855-8616 (Mon. - Thurs. 9am – 5pm Eastern)
E-mail - info@lmw.org • Order online at www.lmw.org

PURPOSE STATEMENT

LEADERSHIP MINISTRIES WORLDWIDE

exists to equip ministers, teachers, and laymen in their understanding, preaching, and teaching of God's Word by publishing and distributing worldwide *The Preacher's Outline & Sermon Bible®* and related **Outline Bible Resources**; to reach & disciple men, women, boys and girls for Jesus Christ.

MISSION STATEMENT

1. To make the Bible so understandable – its truth so clear and plain – that men and women everywhere, whether teacher or student, preacher or hearer, can grasp its message and receive Jesus Christ as Savior, and...

2. To place the Bible in the hands of all who will preach and teach God's Holy Word, verse by verse, precept by precept, regardless of the individual's ability to purchase it.

The **Outline Bible Resources** have been given to LMW for printing and especially distribution worldwide at/below cost, by those who remain anonymous. One fact, however, is as true today as it was in the time of Christ:

THE GOSPEL IS FREE, BUT THE COST OF TAKING IT IS NOT

LMW depends on the generous gifts of believers with a heart for Him and a love for the lost. They help pay for the printing, translating, and distributing of **Outline Bible Resources** into the hands of God's servants worldwide, who will present the Gospel message with clarity, authority, and understanding beyond their own.

LMW was incorporated in the state of Tennessee in July 1992 and received IRS 501 (c)(3) nonprofit status in March 1994. LMW is an international, nondenominational mission organization. All proceeds from USA sales, along with donations from donor partners, go directly to underwrite our translation and distribution projects of **Outline Bible Resources** to preachers, church and lay leaders, and Bible students around the world.

www.ingramcontent.com/pod-product-compliance
Lightning Source LLC
Chambersburg PA
CBHW081230020426
42331CB00012B/3106